Cedar Fence Rows

A COLLECTION OF SHORT STORIES

by

By Georgia Carole Douglas

authorHOUSE®

AuthorHouse™
1663 Liberty Drive, Suite 200
Bloomington, IN 47403
www.authorhouse.com
Phone: 1-800-839-8640

First published by AuthorHouse 5/13/2008

ISBN: 978-1-4343-6765-5 (sc)

Library of Congress Control Number: 2008903372

Printed in the United States of America
Bloomington, Indiana

This book is printed on acid-free paper.

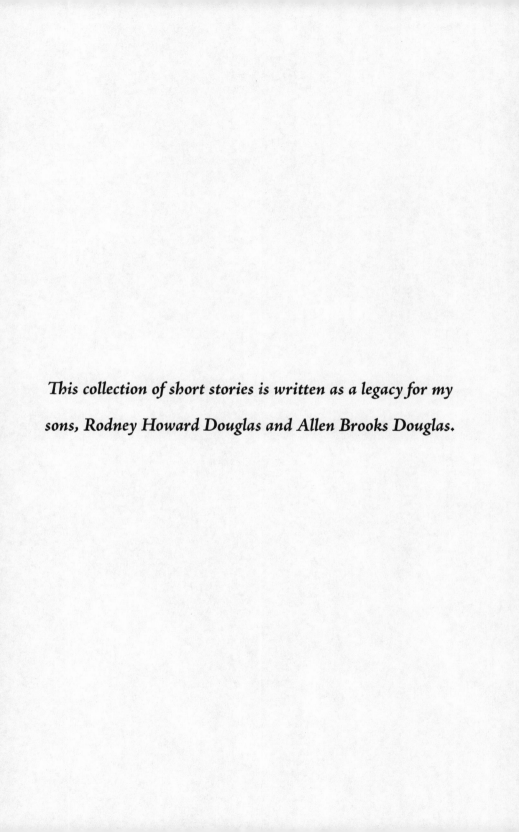

This collection of short stories is written as a legacy for my sons, Rodney Howard Douglas and Allen Brooks Douglas.

In Gratitude

To my darling love, David, a man who touched my heart at age fifteen and then again all these years later. He has become an intricate part of this living journey I am taking. He has taught me so much with his wisdom, his love and his patience. Each day that unfolds continues to bind us together in joy. 'Whatever our souls are made of, his and mine are the same.' – Emily Bronte.

Contents

Author's Introduction

THE FUTURE IS ALWAYS FRESH AND EXCITING, AND IT HAS A PULL ON US THAT TIMES PAST SIMPLY CAN NEVER MUSTER. YET IT MAY WELL BE THAT OUR GREATEST WEALTH AS HUMAN BEINGS CAN BE DISCOVERED BY SIMPLY LOOKING BEHIND US.

FROM THE BOOK 'WISH YOU WELL' BY DAVID BALDACCI

In the time period of writing this book, sometimes I wondered if I indeed was dwelling too long in the past. Upon reading this marvelous book by David Baldacci, I realized that he had expressed my exact feelings! Therefore, I will use his words to express my sentiment.

I send my heart felt appreciation
to my brother Jerry for pictures and constant encouragement,
and to my wise and caring proof reader, Lisa Boggs

Please Allow Me

Please allow me to introduce myself. I am a southern born, Succulent Wild Women. Growing up in the western most tip of Kentucky in a grand and glorious time, could account for some of my personality. My brother likes to say that our parents went headlong into life. He says they worked hard and they played hard. They were natural born risk takers. I suppose everyone takes for granted, when they are in the growing stages, their surrounding influences. That's because they know no other way.

Our paternal grandmother was 5'8" and fat. She was so fat she had to have help getting up from her little gardening stool during those hot Kentucky summers when we went with her to pick Crowder peas. A fiery Irish woman married to a fiery German man, she simply made the best of things. Her hair was brilliant red and hung down past her behind. She plaited and wrapped it round her head. Pale complexion and watery blue eyes, I loved her...oh I love her but did not want to look like that. To this day when I see a haggard image in the mirror, I say, 'hope I'm not beginning to look like Grandmother.'

I did often wish for the beautiful red hair of several of my cousins. Marion was tall and lithe. She died on my birthday...a compliment to me. She wouldn't have wanted us to mourn her in the traditional way. She always strived to be different from others. A marvelous watercolor painter and a woman who always did things with much drama, everyone she loved will always remember her in a special way. After her funeral luncheon, I danced a tango with her brother in law; we danced to a life worth celebrating.

Her daughter says she can remember her father saying, 'just look at your mother with that red hair and that body, she is so beautiful people stop and stare.'

But, as I wished to have a diamond birth date like Aunt Georgia Lee, wishing for the red hair didn't work either. One time as a wild and free grown up in California, I got it out of a bottle. It wasn't the same.

Our daddy was tall, big and strong-minded. Let me tell you! He came home from Europe after World War II and never slowed down to much more than take a breath. He and mother each had their own businesses and they were just as spicy an emotional mix as our grandparents. Maybe more. They loved to argue and they loved to dance.

Our school was so very special and I think I always knew that. It was a lab school that served as training for prospective teachers, located right on the college campus. I had only to walk about three city blocks and I was there.

We were educated within a strict but inspiring environment. Looking back, we know now that each was directed in their own way. I think you've already realized that I'm an incurable romantic. I blossomed in English, Music, Speech and Drama. My friend Paula blossomed in Science and Math. She says she never could conjugate verbs. I could conjugate all over the place but almost dropped in a dead faint trying to pass an Algebra test.

I could write an entire book about that school and how we were exposed to Shakespearean drama and had to learn to swim in high school. However, this is a story, not a book.. I did mention a strict environment. Oh my! We weren't allowed to slow dance, only square dance and be very careful about touching. My sophomore year there was a gorgeous new freshman boy who pulled me into the hall entrance and kissed me silly. Sparks flew!! And the principal caught us.

That mean old man took care of any ideas from us the very next morning in his office. A paddling for the sweet new boy and a stern lecture for me that made me feel guilty to my toes! The handsome boy went on to fall in love with someone else and I went on to have an entire covey of boyfriends. However, we did sing in chorus together and form a bond of friendship. As the high school years flew by, oh so often he seemed to be there, just looking at me. That darling fair-haired boy!

Our parents, the times, the town and our school molded us into unique individuals.

To say that Daddy was strict with me would be an understatement! Many times I thought he was downright mean. Now I know that I could be dauntless, stubborn and fiery in my own defense. I have been told that I am most persistent and strong willed. I say it's Daddy's fault and I'm proud.

Tender hearted. Oh I have a squishy soft heart. Now in the evening glow of my life, I tell people that my first purpose is to reach out and love. To make people feel good, to give them peace. I am a dunked southern Baptist girl. Left my parents Methodist Church in search of something different and I found it there in my little church. I don't always agree with the 'Convention' ideas, but am president and general manager of the Dr. 'Brother' Jim Simmons fan club. He was our preacher, our minister at the church for twenty years. I only had the honor of hearing his sermons for a few years before he resigned and began a new life. What a great man of God!

How grand the feeling to walk into the building where I found my spiritual life at age twelve. To have the memories of so many years is a blessing beyond belief.

Another blessing beyond belief are my growing up girlfriends! There are two left here in my little world that began first grade with me, Catherine and Charlotte. Several more who transferred from other schools to ours in second grade. Classes were so small at our school; everyone became friends with even younger brothers and sisters of classmates. We are together often now and call ourselves, "The Clear Day Girls" cause 'on a clear day, you can see forever'. We've gone on trips, mourned losses, shared joy and wallowed in comfort at slumber parties where we brought heating pads and pain medication and stayed up most of the night, just remembering. And to this day…continue to share love for each other!

I must tell you about my Mother, for I do believe that a great portion of her Cherokee blood runs throbbing through my veins. She was beautiful, only five feet tall, physically, but could rule the roost with her personality. I often clashed with her as I think I am mostly like my daddy and his side of the family. Her side was all affection and emotions. I can say that now, because except for a stray third cousin or two, they are all dead. She was such a flirt and as I reached puberty, that began to embarrass me . She loved a good looking man and let them all know it. Now before you get the wrong idea, she was true blue to my daddy. She liked to dress up head to toe. Wearing a hat, purse and gloves that matched her outfit was her idea of making a heavenly impression. I honestly think that she loved us most when we began our teen-age development. Before that she just didn't seem to know what to do with us. When Daddy came home from the war he about had a stroke. My little brother had long golden curls and mother dressed him in prissy suites. Two days after his return, Daddy took my brother to the barber and had those golden curls sheared off forever. Well actually not forever. When my brother was all grown up and became a wonderful artist, he grew his hair long again and told my mother he had to do it to fit in the 'artistic community.' I'm certain she didn't care, because she loved him beyond degree, I suspect that was said to appease Daddy.

I've done some deep thinking about why I simply enjoy most men. A bit of that may come from mother, but my first male role model was my grandfather on Daddy's side. The fiery German. I adored him! Tall, big boned, strong and strong willed, his appearance might intimidate upon first meeting, but those who spent time with him came to realize his warmth and substance. White fluffy mustache and thick gray hair parted right down the middle, large hands and feet and as for me, all filled up with love. I loved him so much I used to push my face into his chest and take deep breaths, always getting a tender kiss on top of my head. I'd crawl into his feather bed and say, 'I love the way my Pappy smells.' So kind and patient, he'd let me stand behind him on a wooden box and comb his hair until I got my fill of 'grooming' him. I was four years old and adored him so fiercely. He never called me by name, just called me 'Baby'.

I have heard daddy say that his papa never wanted to wear a suite, but I have a picture of him actually wearing one. I do remember him saying, 'when I die I want to be buried in my favorite clothes, a new long sleeved white dress shirt and a pair of 'new blue' overalls.'

Saying he was too old and set in his ways to learn driving a car, he went to town in his wagon, proudly pulled by his mules, Kate and Dinah.

I used to run up the highway to meet him coming home. He'd lift me astride Dinah and I'd ride barefoot and saddle free all the way to the barn.

In my heart I know he grieved the day that Daddy had to be the brave one and sell them. Daddy had to be the brave many times through out his life.

Grandfather died on a night in June, weeks before my seventh birthday. He went the way he always said he wanted to go away, in his sleep. And in the casket he wore what he had asked to wear. I cried and sang all the way to the little country church in Tennessee. My aunt asked mother to 'make that child be quiet'. My mother said, 'oh leave her be.' My mother loved him fiercely too.

His going away left a vacuum in our lives. Grandmother's red hair turned white as cotton and she had it cut. Losing pound after pound until she became a thin, big boned woman who clung to my father for the rest of her days.

My daddy was a 'rebel with a cause'. He left west Tennessee as soon as he cleared high school. He was a baseball hero there in Cottage Grove. I found a report card one time while digging through an old trunk in the basement. I can tell you this now, he didn't make good grades. He also didn't make a good farmer. Grandfather raised tobacco and sweet potatoes, acres and acres of them and Daddy hated every minute of the process from spring till harvest. He went to Michigan after trying

California. He refused to bend to grandfather's ways and made good money in the car plant. He came home for a visit and to bring money to his parents and that's when he met his 'waterloo'. There was my beautiful mother and she set a net for him. As I've said before, they both worked and played hard. Daddy even sold suites for a company door to door and that began his life of dressing up. Unlike grandfather, he loved a suite and hat. I had friends in school that thought he was a mafia man. He often wore dark pin stripes and always that 'fedora'. I think some of that had to do with my grandfather's overalls. He sold everything he could sell and was good at it too. For several years he sold beef cattle, sheep and goats. Produce and suites came in his early life. He most enjoyed selling cars and always had a gently used Cadillac for the family car. In his twilight life he was town Santa Claus for years and as I say in poetry, that was his favorite of all occupations.

The idea to refer to myself as a 'Succulent Wild Woman' came from a card I found while shopping in friend Gwynn's little hometown of Dickson, Tennessee. We were having one of those girlfriend weekends and they are always grand. This card says a succulent wild woman should be "delicious…eat mangoes naked, lick the juice off your arms…discover your own goodness…smile when you feel like it…be rare eccentric and original…describe yourself as marvelous….paint your soul…make more mistakes…tell the truth faster…celebrate your gorgeous friendships with women…. dress to please your self…be inwardly outrageous…. bathe naked by moonlight…you are enough, you have enough, you do enough….let your creative spirit rush, flow, tumble, leap, spring, bubble, stream, dribble out of you"… By Sark. That sounded so much like me, even though I could add a few more. Given my ancestry and growing up environment, I think it's easy to believe. Oh, I can still conjugate verbs, but don't always choose to do so.

Memories of Mammy

Tonight as I sat down to my solitary evening meal, memories of the past swept through my mind - so strong, sweet and welcomed. Remembering meals years ago at home, when we all gathered around the table. In spring, summer and autumn time we ate on the glass-enclosed back porch overlooking the yard. There was a long, narrow wooden table and ample room for all. My paternal grandmother lived with us and I think those times were best. She had a way of calming my dad's insecurities. Now before you get any ideas that my dad was more insecure than most, I've come to realize that isn't true. All parents with the heavy responsibility of making a living and raising kids, have to feel insecurities! It happened generations before and it will happen generations to come. The kind of reactions depends upon the personality. At least that's what I think. My grandmother was a nurturer pure and simple. She'd raised her five children and several others long before my brother and I came along, just two more little ones, needing her.

She was completely dependent upon my parents for absolutely everything. I can remember hearing her say that if it weren't for us she would be living at the 'Poor Farm'. These were times of no social security and for all of her life she had known only the farm until my grandfather could no longer cash rent. They had lost a large tobacco and sweet potato farm in the depression. However, that dependency did not make her weak. She had a strong and lasting effect upon our lives and daddy gleaned from her a sense of homing.

For years I was embarrassed to call her Mammy in front of my friends. Daddy called her Mama and everyone else called her Mammy. I now know that in Ireland among the commoners, the mothers are called Mam and the grandmother's Mammy. She kept very little of her Irish heritage, blending with a great love into my grandfather's German ways.

I have no memory of the time when I was taken to my grandparents to live. I must have been very young. There are things I remember well, living in the big farmhouse with them : kerosene lamps, a battery radio, coal burning fireplaces, feather beds, hot bricks in bed on a cold night, a big barn, cattle, mules and chickens, and going with my older cousins to drop the bucket down into the well for delicious, cold water. And I will never forget Mammy's fluffy white coconut cakes, chess pies, cornbread and biscuits, all baked to perfection on a wood-burning cook stove. She prepared three full meals a day, canned and made sour kraut and hominy in season. Everything grown in the big garden was 'put up' or eaten in summer. I can still see her moving her big body out the back door with rapid grace, grabbing a chicken by the neck and wringing off the head for frying or making dumplins.

When Daddy came to say goodbye before he was shipped to Europe during World War 11, I remember crying so passionately and begging him not to leave. He gave me his GI shoeshine kit and told me to keep it for him until he came back home to us. Mammy was especially attentive to me for several days after Daddy left to ship out to Europe. I know she must have been troubled and sad, but she kept her feelings hidden away.

As I have told in another story, Mammy was a big, fat woman with bright red hair. She wore Emma Jettick shoes, the black, substantial lace-up style, ordered from a traveling salesman, floral dresses and, the almost ever-present apron. Her neighbor friends came occasionally to quilt on a large frame in the living room. I loved to crawl underneath and watch the tiny, perfect stitches appearing in the color patchwork.

When she and I were alone she taught me to dance and sing. 'Skip To My Lou My Darling' was our dancing song and 'You Are My Sunshine' was our harmonizing song. She could be so much fun but oh my, so strict. My little legs got the hickory switch when I didn't behave, and I will admit there were times when I was ornery. I suppose that was all a part of eventually becoming a 'succulent wild woman'.

As a teen I was my daddy's shadow. Whatever he was doing, I gladly tagged along to help. Often that meant helping heard the cattle or hogs down the loading chute, taking bales of hay from top the truck, or filling the large water tank inside the barn. Mammy would say to him, ' Lord have mercy son, you are turning that girl into a tomboy, this has got to stop!' Her prediction didn't come true. I am mostly a 'girly girl' but can do a lot of things out of necessity. The day my new boyfriend came to call and caught me outside covered in mud, herding errant hogs and smelling like one, she said, 'I told you so'. I never heard from him again, but it didn't bother me one tad. I found another soon thereafter, even more handsome.

I do believe that those suppers around the table with every family member present, the front porch visits, family reunions and cousins sleeping on pallets on the floor, were wonderful bonding experiences so important in the making of the people we became.

Just as I know Mammy loved me, to this day I wonder at all the energy she summoned from deep inside her heart and soul. And I am ever so thankful for all of it!

DADDY SOMEWHERE IN EUROPE DURING WORLD WAR II
I SAID A PRAYER FOR HIM AND KISSED THIS PICTURE EVERY SINGLE NIGHT UNTIL HE RETURNED IN DECEMBER OF MY SIXTH YEAR

The Griffin Place

There exist nowhere in my memory the time I was taken to my grandparents house to live. Goodness, I must have been very young, because I remember my mother taking me to the Love's photography studio for a picture of my first birthday. She placed my blanket upon a table for a make shift cloth and put the big cake with its single candle in the middle. Then she sat me on a stool, all primped for the picture. The small amount of hair I had managed to grow was combed up into what grandmother called a 'top knot'.

I remember wanting to put my finger into that cake but knowing I had best not yield to the temptation.

That adventure with my mother was just that - a visit. I lived with my paternal grandparents on a farm a few miles out from town. We called it 'The Griffin Place' because absolutely everything except the furniture, our clothes and the livestock, belonged to Mr. Griffin. My grandfather had previously owned a large sweet potato and tobacco farm in west Tennessee. Pappy as we all called him told the story many times of how they lost everything but their personal items to a cruel, wealthy creditor who owned most of their little town of Cottage Grove. Now let me tell you, cash was severely limited in those days. Cash money was usually obtained only once a year. When the crops were sold at harvest time and all the bills were paid, if anything was left, that was the cash money that must last until the next year. Pappy always said that Mammy charged too often and too freely at the general store. He said she was also high minded and wanted fancy things for their three daughters. Of course, those things were charged at the local store. The cruel creditor foreclosed and took everything away. Pappy always told this story when Mammy was not in the room. However, Mammy never had a story and wouldn't talk about it. I do know that my aunts did have beautiful things because the one who survived into old age often talked about the beautiful clothes they wore.

So from the time I could remember, we lived on a rented farm. Pappy ploughed the fields walking behind a singletree plough pulled by one of his two mules. There was a big barn behind the house with a fenced lot. We had milk cows, pigs, mules and chickens. No electricity or running water. Oil lamps lit the house and Mammy cooked elaborate meals upon a wood fired cook stove. The bedrooms upstairs were not heated. Each bed had a feather bed and lots of quilts. In winter Mammy put a heated brick in the bed to make it cozy. She ironed all our clothes with flat irons heated on the wood stove and we had a battery radio that was only turned on twice a week, once for the news and on Saturday night to listen to the Grand Ole Opry from Nashville. Water was brought into the house from the well. The iceman delivered big blocks of ice that were placed in what was called an icebox.

Mr. Griffin came once a month to visit and talk with Pappy. Mammy always served him a sumptuous dessert. I was told to be quiet and polite to him. One day while exploring in the woods that joined the yard on the south side, I found a quaint little house hidden in among the trees. Looking into the window I marveled at the beautiful things inside. That night during supper I asked Pappy and Mammy about the people who lived in the house I had discovered. They both told me I must not go back there because that was Mr. Griffen's house. I said, 'does he live there?' and they said no, he visits there. Oh my, that puzzled me! The next time Mr. Griffin drove up in his shiny black car, all dressed up in suite and tie, I sat looking at him and thinking he was so handsome and he smelled nice too. Soon after he left, my little girl curiosity became overwhelming. I slipped out the back door and walked to the little house. There was the shiny black car, parked by the door. I thought about knocking on the door to see if he would let me inside for a visit. Then I heard a woman's voice. I peaked into the window and saw a beautiful lady dressed in such a fancy nightgown. I didn't understand the entire thing but I knew that Mr. Griffin was probably doing something he shouldn't, and I didn't dare tell my grandparents about what I had seen. When I grew older and began to go to the movies and became a part of many girlfriend talks, I realized just what happened at that little house in the woods and why it remained a deep, dark secret.

The Uncle I Loved

While walking with a friend the other day she mentioned how she loved one of her uncles as a young girl; and how he added so much substance and thrill to she and her sister's small girl world. That conversation put me in mind of my favorite uncle and moved me to tell about him. Because he was such an incredible man, I owe him the honor of preserving his loving ways for posterity and hopefully motivating some young uncles to leave an unforgettable legacy to their nieces and nephews.

Try as I may, I cannot remember my age when I first became aware of Uncle A.B. The initials stand for Alvin Bernard Dunn II. Which makes it obvious why he preferred his initials! He was my mother's youngest brother and came into our lives with quite a checkered history.

He was so young when their father died very suddenly. They were one of the well to do families in the little town of Hazel, Kentucky. Grandfather Dunn worked for the railroad and that meant a substantial income for those times. Mother used to tell the story of how she was born in Crossland, a town even smaller than Hazel, in a rented house that sat on the state line between Tennessee and Kentucky. The living room was in Tennessee and the bedroom where she was born, in Kentucky. As my grandfather matured and went to work for the railroad, they built a beautiful two-story house off the main street of Hazel and were the first family to own a motorcar. Uncle Guy was the oldest child, then my mother, Violet and Uncle A.B. was the baby of the family.

When grandfather died suddenly of renal failure, the family was on the mercies of the world. Grandmother became ill and they lost all of their possessions. Placed lovingly in my mother's curio cabinet are two etched candleholders, all that she had of her mother possessions after everything else was sold. Mother moved the family to Murray and began working as a waitress in a hotel restaurant. She was a divorced woman with a daughter, an ill mother, and two brothers, dependent upon her. The stigma of divorce weighed heavily upon her determined spirit but it didn't stop her from long hours of work. With very little adult supervision, Uncle A.B. grew to be a wild child. Even though he was a high school football hero, dubbed Dynamite for his speed and skill on the field, he skipped school so often, he never graduated. His handsome face, well-developed body and loads of charm were not wasted upon a local girl whose father owned the butcher shop.

In those days to own a business was a symbol of prestige. Her family disapproved of A.B. and his poor background; his social standing was not good enough for their daughter. My mother's family was so poor, when my grandmother died, my mother did not have enough money to pay for her funeral. She begged a local funeral parlor owner, the largest in town, to allow her to pay him monthly until the debt was satisfied. He refused, but thankfully a smaller owner allowed her to have the funeral there. Soon thereafter, Uncle A.B. and Neal ran away and got married. World War ll came all too soon for the newly wedded couple. Uncle A.B. was drafted and sent to the South Pacific and then on to Europe in areas of raging battles. He saw Mussolini hanged just before being shipped home.

Haunting memories of battle and the increasing pressure from his wife's unhappy family seemed to trigger his inherited propensity to alcoholism. When he first came to live with us, the marriage had ended and he was drinking almost constantly. Even with this deep personality defect, he was one of the most passionate, loving persons I have ever known. He drove a produce truck throughout the region, delivering to little country stores. For this he stayed sober and often took my brother with him.

He liked bringing home gifts for us, and his kind of gifts were far from ordinary! The unique treasures gladdened the hearts of a little boy and girl. A pet goat one time and a 1939 Ford Coup were among the things I remember best. I learned how to drive with that old car in the field behind the barn. I could talk to him about anything and he understood my feelings. I was despondent about a new boyfriend's lack of attention and told him all about it, sobbing my fourteen year old heart out. He told me to come get in his car; we were going for a ride. He was so handsome; all my girlfriends were agog over him. He had me sit close to him and we drove by that boys house once, turned and drove by again. How I laughed when the boy called all upset over my new, older man!

In the early fifties he met a woman eighteen years younger than he, and after a whirlwind courtship, they were married. My dad in all his wisdom saw this as A.B.'s opportunity for a fresh start. He gave them a 1951 Cadillac, bedding, money and sent them to Texas with the sage advice to get jobs and begin a new life. My Uncle A.B. often said years later that I prayed him into sobriety.

I did pray often for him and with him, but I truly think it was the new start in Texas and his great love for a dedicated, wonderful wife whose love for him was passionate and unequivocal. Anna became a loving and important member of our family. Alvin Bernard Dunn II, did get a good job, joined AA and later became a Mason and a Shriner. Four children were born to their union and as I witnessed his deep love for them, I realized part of why he was such a wonderful uncle to us.

Our Drum Major

'Long ago but not so very long ago
the world was different, oh yes it was
You settled down and you built a town
And made it there
You watched it grow, it was your town.

Time goes by, time brings changes,
You change too…..

Lyrics from the song 'Our Town' by James Taylor

As the song goes ' long ago but not so very long ago' I was living my teen years in our little town - population 8,000 and growing ever so slowly. I was yet to become the 'Succulent Wild Woman' I am today. In fact, I was a sometimes shy and reticent girl. Within the reflective wisdom of aging, I know now that I often doubted my intellect and beauty, despite my mother telling me I was such a lovely girl/woman. I'd think, 'She's my mother, she's supposed to think that way.'

My brother and I were students at the high school on the college campus, but we had scores of friends who lived inside the city limits and went to the downtown high school. Our school had many advantages; among them were an orchestra, swim classes in the college pool and live production plays on campus. Our teachers were on the college faculty.

We were archrivals of the city school. Some of their students teased us and called us 'Guinea Pigs'. In truth we were an experimental school, but a wonderful one. In their immaturity they didn't realize that, and in our immaturity, we allowed it to bother us greatly. All this being so, we who admired them did it rather quietly. Our colors were blue and gold; their colors were black and gold. We were the Colts, but they were the Tigers. They had a football team and a marching band.

These days along with wisdom and age, I have learned to give in to my emotional motivations and believe me, I experience lots of them. They come as often as menopausal hot flashes to a middle-aged woman! When emotions move me, I like to share the reason why.

I went into the insurance office one day to visit with my friend Glenda, pay my bill, and visit some more. I do this as often as I have an excuse to, and Glenda and I reminisce all over the place! This particular day she asked if I remembered the Murray High School drum major from our days, Boogie Thurman. Oh, of course I did! And my emotions have moved me to tell about him.

What teen-age girl in town or out of town, who stood on the Main Street sidewalk for a parade, could forget that site? Some of us girls never missed a town parade and often attended the city football games. Being invited to the dance after a city football game was an especially delicious experience as dancing was not allowed at our school parties

We were typical teens of the fifties, wearing black skirts, pink and black tops, bobby socks and saddle shoes or penny loafers. Handsome boys were considered 'dreamy' and sighed over at every opportunity. Standing on the sidewalk feeling the drum beat of the approaching band was like experiencing a huge heartbeat all over your body! Then 'he' would come down the street leading the band, -shoulders back, head up with that wonderful tall hat a top his blonde hair, legs stepping so high they cut the air in two with each kick. It seemed that the only time his warm, golden brown eyes weren't smiling was when he carried out the awesome responsibility of leading that band right through the center of town. Every movement in perfect time, he looked like a man out of the movies to we girls with raging hormones and fluttering hearts.

It was rumored that he never had to search for attention from a girl. Most of them would gladly jump at a chance for time with him and many did. And even though I dated an older boy on the city football team for a time, I was always too awed to even think about a chance to hold his hand or have an after school coke date. If he had ever asked I would have likely fainted on the spot.

No one was surprised a few years later when the marriage announcement came out in the paper. Our drum major had married the sultry, vivacious Elsie Love. Her family owned the local photography studio just one block south of Main Street off the square.

Years passed by. Eventually I left town with my college degree and much trepidation, seeking to begin a new life in the big, outside world.

One time while visiting home I looked as I drove by and saw a sign that said 'Thurman Ballroom Dance Studio'; instantly I knew that the drum major and his Elsie were teaching dance. Our drum major's first name was Charles but no one called him that. They always called him 'Boogie'. He said it was because he danced on the piano bench while his sister played boogie-woogie songs; they began to call him that when he was two years old. I personally think the man was born with music in his soul.

Years of abundant joy and sorrow have transpired for everyone since the long-ago days of innocent crushes. Sorrow brought me home again after spending the interim years living in other places. Dear friends soon found me and reached out, in love and friendship to invite me to a dance. There they were, Boogie and Elsie, welcoming me home. After many lessons from both of them, I now take the floor to waltz lightly within his arms. I reference dear Boogie in poetry, saying, 'In admiration and respect, I borrow him for the measure of a song, returning him where he belongs, Unscathed except for the joy of a single dance, and his grace.'

A mutual friend saw me the other day in an antique store and began to talk of the last time he saw Elsie. We were reminiscing and grieving her recent death. 'Someone tapped me on the shoulder,' he said, 'and I turned around face-to face with her - dressed in animal print from head to toe, there she was with strawberry hair that blended to the colors of her gorgeous clothes. Bracelets, rings and earrings in place - tangerine lipstick and nail polish - every single thing about her was vibrantly coordinated, as always. Suddenly everything and everyone around blended to black and white and she, in vivid color, takes center stage in my mind's eye. That will always be my memory of her.' Ben continued his story of reunion, informing me that Elsie hadn't changed a bit even though she had been ill for a long time. 'Oh she was still just as strong willed, opinionated, and flamboyant, wasn't she? And out spoken too, but then that was Elsie through and through.'

Though everyone who knew her realized that she possessed these characteristics, I also believe that she developed the art of glittering like Las Vegas - inside and out- to capture and keep the heart of our glorious, marching Main Street drum major.

'Time goes by, time brings changes, you change too, nothing comes that you can't handle, so on you go, Never see it coming, the world caves in on you on your town. Nothing you can do....Main Street isn't Main Street anymore....but it's our town, love it anyway, Come what may, it's our town.'

Poetry quote from the book 'Moon Stages' Heart Dance page 49

The Demon Of Self Righteousness

I was just fifteen years old when I came to experience the demon of self-righteousness. In my opinion that is much too young, but fate gave me no choice.

Most of my stories are filled with humorous incidents and certainly to overflowing with love, all kinds of love. This story isn't pretty but it's been on my heart for fifty-two years, and I simply must tell it.

Now there are self-righteous people all over the world, have been since time began. However, here in the South, smack in the middle of the Bible belt, it seems to grow as easily as mold. The difference being, it is much more insidious!

I came to know God at the tender age of twelve. I've mentioned growing up in my mother's church. Even that young, I seemed to realize that I didn't think I fit there. It was just a feeling that grew stronger with time. A new friend at school invited me to their church. She told me of the young Canadian minister. Everyone thought his sermons were wonderful. From the first time I heard Brother Sam preach, I was changed. I knew I had truly met a man of God. And everything in that church just seemed to 'fit' for me.

Soon thereafter, or anyway it seemed not long, I began to feel as if my parents were just too busy. I know now that a part of that feeling was the beginning of my teen-age change and up roaring hormones.

The parsonage was a pleasant walk from our house and I spent a lot of time there with Mrs. B, Brother Sam and their two sons. I found friends, jobs to do and my heart felt home.

My daddy had bought our house just after his military discharge in 1947. It was Mother and Daddy's 'dream come true' home…an upper and lower yard with many old shade trees, a cattle barn in back with a pond, an old orchard and a garden space. A grand place for my brother and I to play. Daddy added to the magic by acquiring most any pet we desired. A gentle old horse, a dog, several barn cats and pet goats. Mother planted rose bushes and flowers all around the yard. I thought the place just heavenly and Daddy would say, 'it's all our own!'

Every summer we had family visitors. Mother's aunt from Texas always came to stay a while. What a lady! She had been raised in Tennessee but married a Texan and lived in Pecos. Now if you've ever been to west Texas, you know why my great Aunt Betty loved to come to Kentucky in summer. She would say, ' My name is Betty Isora Duncan Smotherman Myers and I'm proud to meet you'. Grandmother's sister came each year also. She lived in Little Rock where her husband worked for the railroad. She was a little over five feet tall and almost every bit as round as that. Laughing eyes and a loving heart, she would say, 'Child you are beautiful and oh how I've missed you!' Both greats always attended church with me during their visits with the family.

Our property was separated from the neighbors to the north by a large ditch over which someone had placed a bridge. Elmer and Ina owned the immediate house. Just next door to them lived their son and daughter in law, Edgar and Stella. Of all those people, I only felt warmed by Ina. She was a dear little lady in her late seventies. Around Elmer she was quiet and shy, but when she came to visit grandmother she seemed to blossom. Edgar and Stella were angry, loud spoken people who made me uncomfortable. Being a child, I kept my feelings to myself. I can remember my mother complaining in a humorous way that Stella lacked manners and never knocked when she came visiting -just barged right in the door. Edgar enjoyed being the center of attention and would talk on and on about his salvation, often quoting scripture. It seemed to my little girl mind that he was critical of almost everyone.

When I found my church, guess who were prominent members? Yes, both those families. Edgar was a deacon and Elmer was currently 'resting' from years of deacon service.

In the spring of my fourteenth year a story swept town and everyone was talking about the two run away girls from somewhere up north. Our little town knew nothing of social workers or Children and Family Services. Brother Sam and family were asked to take these girls into their home. The girls would not tell the police anything about themselves, only that they were afraid to be sent back home.

They were enrolled into the city school system and I attended the college school. However, I spent numerous hours with them at church activities and knew that they were so happy to be accepted and feel safe.

Wasn't long until several people began to tell stories. Gossip flew back and forth like acid rain. Twenty-five people in my church called a special meeting and demanded that Brother Sam resign and leave town.

I was old enough to know that Brother Sam preached sermons with ideas a little different and he had opinions that weren't of the ordinary old south ideas. One night in the midst of all the poison controversy, Brother Sam and Mrs. B asked me if I would like to ride to the next little town, Paris, Tennessee, with them to pick up two church members at the train station. I gladly went along. The girls and I sat in the back seat and Mrs. B and the boys up front with Brother Sam. Remember the big cars back then? Room for all of us and more. Of course we girls were teen age skinny and the boys were little then.

Brother Sam had just driven into the outskirts of town when a car began following close behind, dimming and brightening its headlights. This car followed us all the way to the edge of the next town, continuing the distracting behavior. To calm our fears, Brother Sam assured us that he knew who it was and why they were doing this. He said, 'I recognize the car, it's Edgar and some of his cronies.' My heart began a pounding! I stayed quiet but my mind was 'going in sixties'! Edgar was so self-righteous, how could he possibly be doing something like this?

The next evening at the dinner table Daddy related the story heard in town. Church members had caught Brother Sam taking those two young girls to Paris, Tennessee to a 'honky tonk'! I cried and cried and told my daddy what had happened. He and Mother consoled me and told me just to keep the story to myself and not get involved.

The situation went downhill from that time. The girls were taken away from Brother Sam's family and placed into another home. Heartbroken, they confessed that they had run away from Chicago, to escape an abusive family member. They consented to be returned home. A church business meeting was scheduled and Brother Sam was confronted with lie after lie. I remember the entire front of my stylish fifties circular skirt was soaked with tears. Even if I had not been so near to this family, I would have never believed those lies. My young heart was broken with disappointment and grief. I did not comprehend such evil could be present in my world. And then I knew the awful demon of self-righteousness, I had stared it in the face and it had shattered lives and hearts.

The day of his last goodbye, Brother Sam stood with me at the empty front entrance of the church. He looked me straight in the eyes and asked me to promise him that I would continue to support the church and not to be angry with God for these things. He also promised that God would heal our hearts and chastise the wickedness.

Twenty-five members left our church and joined another, our trouble making neighbors were among the twenty five who kept rumors alive until Brother Sam and family moved miles away to eastern Tennessee.

One lazy summer afternoon while in my cozy yard, Elmer exposed himself to me. Calmly waiting until Daddy got home was not easy but it is what I did. When I told Daddy about the horrible experience, he calmly got up from his chair and went out the back door to cross the bridge. I never knew what Daddy said or did to Elmer, but Elmer never bothered me again. Each and every one of those twenty-five people ended up having horrible experiences. Stella became prescription drug addicted and ran her car into a storefront. Edgar died of a heart attack while driving his tractor.

Elmer lived to be an old, old man. Mother and I attended his funeral, Daddy quietly refused to go. Mother and Daddy lived in their house until they died, in their early nineties. My children and nephews played wonderful hours in that sheltered yard.

At age twenty, I graduated from college and moved to California. I have always known since then that I stared the demon in the face and with God's infinite grace over came evil. My faith has kept me safe and strong and forever in my memory I shall carry one particular verse I heard for the very first time, quoted by Brother Sam....' Under the Shadow of Thy Wings.....

'How excellent is thy loving kindness, O God!

Therefore the children of men put their trust under the shadow of thy wings.

They shall be abundantly satisfied with the fatness of they house;

And thou shalt make them drink of the river of thy pleasures.

For with thee is the fountain of life: in thy light shall we see light." Psalms 36 7-9

From the book Cedar Fencerows Lakeside May 2006

The Training School

Looking back on my childhood, I now know just how blessed I was growing in times of tender concern. In retrospect, I realize that I was born and grew within a protected place, even for that seemingly peaceful portion of history. Becoming a teen in the fifties, in our small town, I experienced profound innocence. Murray was, and still is considered a small town by most standards. Population 10,000, we were told that for absolutely years and years even when the town had actually grown a bit larger. The area has become a magnet for retirees. These days we 'sixty something's' are together often. We are blessed to be retired and living, once again, in close proximity.

Now we can revel in knowledge we did not possess 'back then. It seems a misfortune Children cannot realize and appreciate their surroundings until they have the ability to reflect upon them later in life. I asked a dear friend recently what made our lives so much more peaceful than people of today. She said, 'I think it is because we led such undiluted lives'. How sheltered our lives, as we grew and unfolded, compared to the world of today

Our school was extremely unique, even for those days. We attended a college lab school. Yes, we were a living experiment. Walk with me in your mind and we will explore the physical aspects of that building. Our three-story building, containing a full basement, was located directly on the campus of Murray State. There were three main entrances on the ground level and one back entrance on the basement level. Large, wide hallways were flanked on either side with classrooms and two large bathrooms, one for boys and one for girls. The main floor also contained a principals office, restroom and meeting rooms for faculty. Each classroom consisted of a large main area and a coat or 'cloke room' as we called them. All classrooms contained three to four small rooms for specialized use. The basement area was flanked on one side with a large cafeteria where students and faculty ate lunch and on the other side with a recreation room. A stairwell and breezeway divided the two areas. The main classrooms were spacious and served as the meeting area for the beginning and ending of the day. It was also where classes were held when we were 'observed' by college students. The upper third level consisted of a large music room, art department and home economics department. The school provided instruction for grades one through twelve.

Each year was divided into two semesters. Each one provided new 'student teachers'. We called them practice teachers as they were practicing to become full time teachers upon graduation from the college.

In the early seventies our building was torn to the ground. There was a concern in the city school system that our University school was taking students from their system. The 'powers that be' at that time, decided they must do all they could to close our school. Finally a Federal Fire Marshal came from Washington D.C. and condemned our three story brick building, deeming it a fire hazard. In the battle to keep the school, a new one was built on the site but only remained open for a few more years.

All who attended that grand place agree that we received an unprecedented education. In the near future, there will be exhibits built in the museum on campus, and an area reserved in the historical library for published graduates. These things in honor of the revered memory of that time period; and we who spent those formative years within it's shelter will finally have a history.

Training School Building of Murray State Teachers' College, Murray, Ky.

The Birdfoot Violet

In the movie 'Hearts In Atlantis' the narrator talks about when you are a child, summers seem to last forever. He also says, 'sometimes the past comes flying at you out of nowhere and the only thing you can do is hope it takes you where you want to go.' Happens to me quiet often these days and I have chosen to share those 'visits' with others through my writing.

Approaching the tender of age of sixteen or so, I'm not certain, as that was so long ago. I do remember vividly feeling confused and wanting with all my heart to just feel tenderness and purity. I have mentioned being a Southern Baptist before. At that time in my life the church was the center of my being. And I later realized, although it was my saving grace, a part of it was the center of guilt that would linger with me for years.

And I remember well all those long summers that seemed to last forever. One particular summer, a young cousin of our minister came visiting from Memphis. We had a long, enchanting time together through those warm, sunny days. She invited me to come visit her and, immediately, I decided it was just what I needed. Most of the boys I met seemed interested in only one thing and my immersion in the church certainly didn't allow groping or anything a kin to that favorite boys activity. The church was pressing each and every Sunday that all we young people give our lives in missionary service; and I had begun to think that I must do that very thing in order to please God. I felt so uncertain about where living was going to take me and felt the all too common fearful thoughts that most teens do.

Dad took me to the bus station and I got my ticket to Memphis - feeling so grown up with my adventure. I remember walking to the back of the bus thinking that it would be a grand place to see the road side while riding for the two and a half hours. A black woman told me I couldn't sit there. I asked why and she said, 'well honey this is where they make us sit. The front is for you white folks.' I reluctantly moved and watched the mimosa trees blooming by the roadside and the little towns fly by from my one side window.

Being with Gail and her parents at their home on Mississippi Boulevard was a peaceful and fun experience and the beginning of many visits through the years until Gail decided to get married. One afternoon we walked down the street a few blocks to the Rosewood Pharmacy for a cherry coke. It was there I met a boy younger than I, but oh so sweet. In poetry I call him the blue-eyed soda jerk. He says to this day that it was love at first site for him. I was struck by his tender, caring, polite manner. And thus began a long distance romance. Now in all honesty, I was never in love with him, though his adoration and reassurances were a pure balm to me. We wrote letters and he sent me his signet ring to wear on a chain around my neck. He even came with Gail and her parents to my high school graduation ceremony.

College began the next autumn and with it, new exciting experiences. I had seen a boy when I was sixteen and fallen so entranced by him. He was a Korean War veteran in college on the G.I. Bill and living at a rooming house up the street. In my young girl's mind he had become my prince. The more I tried to win even a look, a smile from him, the more he avoided me. The first week of my freshman year in college he finally approached me walking home and asked me for a date. Letters still came from the Memphis boy and I began to feel guilty about no longer rushing to read his letters at the end of the day. Finally I wrote to tell him that what we shared was over and he should move on to find another to love. Soon thereafter, I had lost my virginity to a rogue of a man in a disastrous affair. As I say in the poem 'There Are Those'; ' he crushed the blossom of love that freely lived in this young girl's heart, until only the fragrance of bruised petals remained. I walked away carefully holding the fragrance.' All my thoughts of 'full time Christian Service' had vanished and I felt as if Gods approval had left me too.

Upon graduation I moved to California, longing to get as far away as possible from home, the prince, who treated me like a sister, an over protective Dad, my guilty experiences. In December, the prince who had always kept in touch by phone and letters, proposed to me. We were married thirty-five grand years when death came and took him from me.

In the midst of grieving and moving toward a new life, an email came from the blue-eyed soda jerk. He had found me on the Internet and thus began a renewal of friendship. I was writing my second book and needed a quiet away place to be. He suggested Doe Run Inn in Brandenburg, Kentucky -a beautiful old stone mill turned hotel and restaurant, in the middle of a tranquil wood. I took his advice and checked in for a week. 'The resident writer', as the management referred to me. My beautiful room was furnished with antiques, void of radio, television or telephone. Downstairs was a delightful restaurant where I ate quiet meals, whenever I chose. Inspiration came and writing the poems I wanted to include in this work seemed to come effortlessly each day.

My ' Memphis Man' visited while I was there and we walked among the spring wildflowers blooming everywhere. I found a tiny Birdfoot violet and he dug it up for me to take home. Those little violets are rare, tender and not easy to transplant and keep. I brought it home and very carefully put its little feet in mossy soil under an elm tree. Tenderly kissed it and asked it to live. There it grows today, four spring times later, bearing beautiful blossoms. I think of my 'Memphis Man', the blue-eyed soda jerk, as a rare and glorious Birdfoot violet. He graces my world in friendship, prayer and assurance, just as he once did. He even understands my grand love for David, the darling fair- haired boy from the blush of my youth.

"Be my friend and teach me to be thine." – Ralph Waldo Emerson

English Peas

In some parts of our country they are simply called green peas, or just peas. Here in the South we called them English Peas. I suppose because we grow and consume many kinds of peas, we needed a name to differentiate them. While in the grocery one day not long ago, I had one of the always wonderful visit with my friend and minister, Jim. He was buying several cans of English peas. He mentioned to me that their son Jimmy was home and how he loved those peas. His saying that put me in mind of yet another childhood story.

My brother and I attended a wonderful school on the campus of our town's university. There was a large cafeteria for all students where 'motherly' women cooked everything from scratch. The food was tasty and we were served a balanced, healthy selection of foods every school day. However as kids are prone to be, we were picky about some of the items. I decided early on that the green peas probably wouldn't be good. After all we didn't ever have them at home! Since Mother had a full time business, Grandmother was our cook; and she preferred Crowder peas to the exclusion of all others. One night around the table at dinner I told about thinking I would not like the English peas we had every single Friday of the world for school lunch. My little brother, whom I nicknamed 'Goody Two Shoes', chimed in with a question. ' Have you even tried just one or two to taste and see if you would like them?' I had to answer, 'No, I just don't THINK I would like them. They are green and look gooey to me.' 'Well,' he said, 'that's no reason not to just taste one or two.' He beamed at Mom and Grandmother when he said that, and they smiled. I knew what they were thinking. 'Oh how smart and sweet, our little blond haired boy is always right!' So, the next time they were served, I tasted one. Oh my! Then I ate a spoonful-then all that were on my plate and decided they were quite delicious! What a surprise, they were so sweet and buttery tasting.

Years later at a family gathering, with ' Goody Two Shoes' present, I had brought a dish to share and told that story. Mom, Dad and Grandmother were long gone to Heaven, so at last he told the truth. 'Oh gosh' he said, 'I hated those things but wanted everyone to just think I didn't because I really pulled one over on you!' 'I don't like them to this day!' Then it was my turn to ask, 'Have you ever tasted just one or two?'

A Proper Southern Lady

As I began to grow into puberty, my mother often repeated the 'rules for a proper southern lady' for my edification. A proper southern lady should never walk down the street smoking a cigarette. She should never attend a formal function without her hose and gloves. There were rules of posture and rules of behavior and they went on and on. Even though I tended to be a bit rebellious by nature, these comments seemed to ingrain themselves within my mind.

Many years later my husband and I had moved back home where he became a member of one of the civic clubs. The club was having a fundraiser banquet and I elected to serve on the decorating committee for the chosen evening meal. I spent most of the afternoon, along with several other ladies decorating the meeting room. Then I rushed home to make certain the boys were settled for the evening and quickly dressed for the occasion. As the Prince and I were driving into town from the lake, I suddenly discovered that I had forgotten my panty hose. No proper southern lady should attend any function without her hose! My husband stopped by a store and I ran in to buy a pair, planning to put them on in the ladies room when we arrived. He patiently waited outside the door while I struggled into the newly purchased hose. Immediately I discovered I had chosen ones that were much too short for my legs and bottom. I could stretch them mightily and they reached my waist, only to slip down again. Taking small steps I came out the door and whispered to him about my problem. Being the consummate gentleman, he suggested that he walk me carefully to my seat and I remain there for the duration of the dinner and program. As we approached a table of choice, to our delight, we discovered a couple that were college acquaintances of ours. He had been a football hero and she a beauty queen and they were greatly admired by all of us. I quickly sat down and warmly greeted them. Throughout the evening, my dear Prince waited on me… bringing my coffee, water and food and graciously asking which salad or dessert I preferred. We soon discovered that our much-admired couple apparently was experiencing a 'rough patch' in their relationship. She kept complaining to him about one thing or another as the evening went along. Finally she said to him in extreme exasperation, 'Well, if you were as loving as he is to her, maybe I'd be a bit happier with you!' 'He waits on her hand and foot and I'd like to know what she does that I can't seem to do for you!'

The Prince and I could hardly contain our amusement, but remained polite and cordial. As the evening ended he took my arm and walked me carefully to the door of the ladies room as the errant hose slid down around the tops of my knees. I stripped off those panty hose and stuffed them into my purse. Leaving the exit door, I breathed a sigh of relief, and stepped into the darkness where no one could tell I was exposing my bare legs to God and all creation.

Times have drastically changed and I actually attend church now with bare legs shining. Regardless, I will never forget the night when I thought I must be a proper southern lady and ended up being the envy of a former beauty queen.

Turnip Greens for Supper

Another autumn day has ended with the setting sun and a glorious slipper moon hanging low in the western sky. Just before dusk I walked across the street and picked a mess of turnip greens from the neighbor's garden. Each year Gordon plants them and I watch for them to grow big enough to pick.

As I plucked the tender leaves from greens just big enough to count, I looked all around at the incredible beauty of the sky. This has been a day of wind, rain and then sunshine. Crisp, cool and just beginning to truly be autumn. I wondered at all the years I had enjoyed this time, but realize now that I have always stopped to glorify in the grand beauty of the changing season. As a child I was passionately aware of changing time, changing season. Then I became a busy adult, taken up with trivial consuming duties and commitments. I am thankful at this 'twilight time' of life that I always managed to give a moment or two over to reveling the seasons, the days, nights and changes of the moon. Hanging clothes upon the line, I would stop and look and drink in the beauty around me. Rushing to get nights duties done, look out the window at the moon and the stars. Glancing at the clock in early morning, cooking breakfast, cajoling kids to get ready for school, I would listen for the bird's songs and watch for a moment as the sun blessed a new day. I also took the time and patience to teach our sons to stop, enjoy and wonder at God's world. Their father, my Prince, often showed them little things that some people never notice or seem to care about. He grew up on a farm in Southern Illinois and spent innumerable hours out of doors working and playing.

With each season I planted a vegetable garden wherever we happened to live. Some places were more convenient than others. While living at Bonny View Farm in Independence, Iowa, a grand fenced garden spot came with the rental of the big, glorious house. Other times I just planted in flowerbeds and canned and froze foods from my bounty. I picked or bought many verities of fruits for jams and jellies to eat with the buttermilk biscuits or corn bread. All done in love for my husband and children while teaching full time many of those years.

Now I take all the time I want simply because I have moments, hours if I choose, to reverently observe God's creations. Being ever thankful for this space that I have earned from the past labors.

When darkness comes, I shall have delicious turnip greens for supper. Until the setting sun fills the sky with glory and night comes softly to my world, I must see it all and then have the greens, with onions, and cornbread, and a heart filled with thanksgiving.

Lust In The Neighborhood

If you truly knew my neighborhood ,the word 'lust' in the title would probably cause gales of laughter or perhaps a bit of curiosity on your part. These wonderful people on my street are and always have been as solid and proper as they come. At one point there were two Baptist deacons among us, now we're down to one.

Some thirty years ago when my husband bought this house for me, located overlooking the banks of Kentucky Lake's Blood River Access, our neighborhood was just beginning to age. During that time period the neighbors in our circle were not considered young - all were settled and in their late fifties or early sixties. Our street forms a circle projecting out upon a peninsula of land. There are two houses inside the land locked area and all others are lakefront around the outside perimeter of the street.

The Prince said he bought the neighborhood, as mine is one of the two in the land locked area and the smallest, most humble of all houses here. I was delightfully surprised to learn that I knew the man who lived directly across the street. He was a hero in my childhood days. He sold and raced cars for a large auto company and often won the Daytona 500 races.

The corporation was so impressed by his sales and racing ability, they built a beautiful rambling white brick house for he and his family. The basement was an identical floor plan to the upstairs and they entertained executives who vacationed here in the lakes area. By the time we came along they had bought the house and he had switched from cars to boats for the same company. He was as the old saying goes, a 'cracker jack' salesman, outselling everyone else nationwide.

While settling in from the move, I told the man that he had always been my hero and he said, 'I hope I never fall off the pedestal.' My goodness, little did I know back then what the ensuing years would bring!

I don't want to make light of the years gone by and the grief I have experienced; so since this is a funny story, I'll skip the sad part.

Time came when the racecar driver and I became widower and widow. He had always been a good neighbor and often a helpful hand to my sons through the years. I considered him a dear friend. He began to offer helping in the yard and on occasion came to sit on the porch and talk. During this time period I was in my late fifties and he in his early eighties.

He called one afternoon to tell me he had heard my radio broadcast from the public station and complimented my show. Then said, 'you know, you're alone and I'm alone, there's no reason why we can't enjoy an evening meal together.' I agreed and told him we'd plan on doing just that. Next day he called to ask if I'd ever been to Cherokee Hills for dinner. This was a unique restaurant built in the middle of a huge cattle farm just across the state line in Tennessee. I agreed to go with him for dinner the next night. Our state road was paved over just as it was laid out many years ago. The founding fathers of this portion of the county tried to please property owners by curving around their properties. The road runs between two major state highways for several miles in this eastern part of the county. The southern part of it has even more curves than the northern part.

That evening he came right on time, just across the street and into my driveway behind the wheel of his shiny black Cadillac. I was out to meet him and into to my side of the car before he much more than came to a stop. He chided me for not waiting for him to come to my door. Oh I should have known then…but I can be naive at times.

Off we went on the southerly route to Tennessee. The restaurant was about ten miles down the highway and then we turned onto a narrow gravel road, driving approximately two miles into the farm. When we arrived they had a table ready for us and he said, 'Now darlin, you just order anything your little heart desires. Price is no object.' Not being one to hold back, I promptly ordered an expensive, delicious meal. Conversation was light and he said more than once, 'Ummm this bread has lots of garlic butter, nothing like garlic don't you think?' I said, 'Oh yes it's truly nutritious and good for you.'

After our meal, we walked out into a brightly moon lit night to the car. He began to drive and I was talking a mile a minute about the beautiful moon, the pure bred cattle roaming around such a pasture and how I appreciated such a grand, rural scene. It took a moment for me to realize that he had pulled off the narrow gravel road into an even more secluded lane. The he looked over at me smiling while unbuckling his seat belt and said to my immense surprise, ' I have always had the 'hots' for you and now let's get with it and taste some of this garlic!' Well, I came alive then, pushing against him with both hands saying ' I don't think so, please take me home!' That 'eighty something' Baptist deacon was hearing none of that and just kept coming at me with his garlic breath huffing! So, I said, 'I don't want to hurt you but I can and I will if you don't TAKE ME HOME!!!' This time it began to sink in that I wasn't enamored with his garlic breath and didn't have the 'hots' for him. He reluctantly refastened his seat belt without a word and began to drive. When he turned right entering the southern, hair pen curvy part of our road, he pushed the accelerator to the limit and we were flying around all those curves! He was grinning and driving as I sat calmly quiet. Suddenly he slowed the car and said, 'can't even scare you can I?' I replied, 'No you can't. I'll admit you're still one hell of a driver, but take me home!' Upon arriving home, I got out of that Cadillac and ran into my house and locked myself away. Who would have thought an eighty plus year old Baptist deacon could have possessed so much fortitude?

Sunday Morning
September 24, 2006

A LETTER TO MY BROTHER

I wanted to call you on the telephone but decided I would only cry.

This September morning my body aches and my soul cries out for what will never be again. It has been ten Septembers without my love, my other spirit. One would think after ten, I would cease to have these longings! A portion of me wishes they would cease to be and a portion of me knows they will never go away. My loving husband always protected me from the world. Helped me lovingly with battles I had to fight. Small battles, large battles that comprise, as I say in poetry, 'what living will surely do'.

Strange, the writing of this letter became interrupted by a ringing phone and forgotten until just now, over a month later. And when I spoke to you next day, you said you had been feeling the same, longing sadness. We are partners in loss and emptiness, you and I. Aren't we lucky to be brother and sister? And we are blessed with the passage of time, caring friends and a lovely corner of the world in which to live. We've both been given our artistic talents and, a sensitive nature and, with it, we create and we reach out to comfort and share our hearts with others.

When I am melancholy about all of those who shaped our lives, loved us and cared tenderly and strongly for us, and I long to see them again, I weep. But we must see each day for the grand gift that it brings and praise God for the fortune of having such glorious people in our lives. From our cradle and on through our lives, they to contribute and comprise the man and woman we became. Although they are no longer here to prod us, to protect us, irritate us and make us laugh and give us strength, they are after all 'the rainbow of our days'.

My love, your Sis.

Goodnight Sweet Prince

How grateful am I for my romantic nature! Some people find it necessary to apologize for it, but I have never found the need, only considered it a blessing. The first time I lay eyes on my 'husband to be', that romantic nature was fairly raging within my sixteen-year-old soul. I told my friend Prudence right then and there that some day I was going to marry that man!

She says she thought I was crazy but didn't tell me because she loved me so much. Poetry describes the years of longing and the funny things I did to gain just a look from him. That very day when I stood in the street and watched him, taking in his tall stature, his black 'crow's wing' hair, I fell in love and he became my Prince. I describe our wedding as a 'fairy tale' affair. Classical music played on the organ. I had discovered the wondrous ability of it to move my soul and especially wanted the 'Morning' movement from Tchaikovsky's Swan Lake, for when I knew he was my Prince, 'Morning has broken, like the first morning' truthfully expressed my inner feelings.

In our little town I was the first young lady to wear a form fitting wedding gown. Designed by a friend of my mother's, it was simply a glorious thing to behold. Ceremony on a late Sunday afternoon, because Sunday was my favorite day of the week. My mother in law told everyone she knew that when we exchanged vows, she'd never heard any given with more sincerity than ours. Candles softly glowed upon the altar; love and wonder softly glowed within my heart. We kissed and our breaths – our very souls – like the first gentle wind of springtime, became one.

He took me on not one, but two honey moons. The first, to northern Michigan, away from the August heat, and the second, in February to the coast of Florida. While taking my turn at driving the beautiful highway around the gulf coast, he asked me who in the world taught me to drive!

And then he began to give me the first of many common sense lessons in survival and living.

For years when we attended weddings, he always kept his arm around my shoulders and held one of my hands. When the vows were read he would gently squeeze my fingertips. Forsaking all others, 'To love and to cherish, in sickness and in health so long as you both shall live?'

The ensuing years would sometimes bring difficulties and trials, but our great love caused us to cling together, where he went I went, forsaking all others and we weathered all the changes and adjustments in our life as one. Little did we know that we would come to vividly live the last portion of those wedding vows, 'in sickness and in health'.

When he slipped away from this life after a long illness, I did not want to live. I am certain anyone who has lost a deep love will agree with me. In the very beginning of the aloneness you often feel as if you do not want to live. Just to go to sleep and not wake up again. And then the conflicting times when you feel as if you cannot get the next breath. And when I began to heal and come alive again, I was convinced that no man would ever love me, look upon me with delight again. There were times when I actually felt as if I had spiritually gone to the crematory with his ashes.

How I commend our sons for their great love to me. Through his illness and ever now, they lift me up in love and care. I told him in our last conversation that he was leaving a portion of himself behind in them. Each time I embrace them or they do some sweetly cherished thing for me, I think of how his great love for me continues through them. And always, always, I praise God for such a legacy!

We spoke of his leaving only one time and talked about a funeral. He did not want one. He asked for a memorial and a testimony to his life. And we did just that. A dear friend of his read my poetry and ended with a quote he felt was a fitting tribute to Raphael Delano's life. Little did he know that my precious Raphael had always been my Prince.

"Now cracks a noble heart, Good night Sweet Prince and flights of angels sing thee to thy rest." -- Horatio's farewell to Homer, Prince of Denmark

William Shakespeare

Space In May – A Love Letter To Heaven

Talking to your spirit Last quarter moon Space in May

They have come
Ladders and chain saws in an old beat up truck
Moving with intent, trees to trim

Dawning cold and gray,
Blackberry winter Grandmother would say
I know you cannot hear
Me
I suppose this is more need inside.. years of habit and depending upon

They are changing the face
Of my dear little space
You bought with a check for star dust and dreaming

Margaret is playing Handle's largo from her room at the top
Almost as if she knows it is -Fitting music for sadness
Change coming from my decisions, my way
And I cannot stop, or hold it at bay

I weep in agony when the dead Dogwood falls
Planted long ago…dug from the woods, small thing
Measure of hope and love and dream
Knowing full well I cannot hold back
The passage of time, living, taking giving
For even though it was dying, A few green leaves remained
Giving grace it's all filled with April blossoms and memories

One hundred twenty dollars with the barter of your ladder
And my heart's tears
Starling reminder of just the years
Gone away like a song
I shall add and I shall build, decisions solely mine
You are not here and have not been for a long, long time
Lost and gone to God's strong arms

Talking to your spirit Last quarter moon Space in May--- 2002

Crossing
A Bridge from Then to Now

Poetry has been a vital part of my life's expressions since I discovered it in school so long ago. I found this anonymous poem and wished that I had been the author of these beautiful thoughts that seemed to be mine. In artist admiration, I pay tribute to the unknown writer and include it here for a farewell to my portion of this book that takes the reader back into my childhood years and my wedding day.

Just as I was confronted with a 'bridge' that I knew I must cross when the Prince gave up his earthly life with me, I shall build a bridge between 'Then' and 'Now' for this book.

Lineage

And sometimes when
I have become
A quiet portrait on the
Wall, will you, my far
Descendant, stop to think
Of me at all?

Suppose your hands are shaped like mine –
You have my nutmeg sense of fun –
Will there be one to tell you so, there,
When my days are
Done?

If you love books,
And fires, and songs,
And slipper moons on Lilac skies,
Toss me a look of shared delight from
Those my own dark
Eyes.
For there is kinship in a curl, and keepsake in a spoken name,
And wine of life may yet be poured
By hands within a frame.

The following poem, I wrote for my beloved…taken too soon, but forever
in my heart. He was my life, and I his, for so many years. In so many
ways I was still a girl when we married. I like to think he taught me well.
Though the void will remain, I live surrounded by love and embraced
by the friendship of the sons we bore. I know this would be his wish for
me.

I also know that he would be immensely proud of the men they have
become.

Letter To Heaven

Oh my dear Prince,
Perhaps there is some way
You can know now
Just how
Our sons have become
Grand men

And then,
Perhaps not
We three like to think
You knew
When your sweet soul
Flew
Home to Heaven
With God

Earthly sod
Became too heavy
For you to bear
Or carry along

Pain and suffering
Kept your lips
From what you wished
To say

You left so peacefully
In such a soft , gentle way
Strangely different
From always being solid and strong
Akin to the notes of
A beautiful
song

A Letter from My First Born Son
The World Traveler

I received this letter in email format from my firstborn. He knows I adore 'seeing' the world through his experiences. He also knows I am extremely proud of him and happy that he is doing the things he's always dreamed of since he was quiet young. Each time we moved to a new town when they were children, I took them to the library, striving to introduce them to my love of libraries and the wonderful world of books.

Of all his letters to me, this is my favorite.

Paris was incredible – I used to think that NYC was the greatest city in the world, but Paris surpasses it by leaps and bounds. I understand now why it's called "The City of Light", you're always submersed in an atmosphere of learning and knowledge while in Paris…be it The Louvre, Notre Dame, or just a café.

Of all the sites I experienced, the Eiffel, Louvre, Notre Dame, Arc de Triumph, the Seine, one in particular was a subtle gem. It's the attraction I'll always remember with the greatest deal of warmth, and that place is Shakespeare & Company. A small bookstore in the Latin Quarter on the banks of the Seine and shouting distance from Notre Dame, it was opened in the 1920's by Sylvia Beach Whitman. It's small, cramped with books, musty in that old bookish way, and the shelves are sagging with decades of weight. Most of the books upstairs are still priced in francs, and there's a nook with an old Royal manual typewriter for anyone's use and a window that looks out over the Seine toward Notre Dame. Local poets still hold readings there.

I was finally able to read 'A Moveable Feast' after trying unsuccessfully a couple times previous. Hemingway speaks so personally of Paris, and it's a tough read if you're not personally familiar with his Paris haunts. Almost all of the places Earnest frequented are still in existence; Café Les Deux Magots, Brasseri Lipp, and of course Shakespeare & Company. Sylvia Whitman loaned books for free to Earnest when he was living in Paris, poor, and struggling to make it as a writer. In the 20's, the bookstore was a hangout for Gertrude Stein, James Joyce, T.S. Eliot, F Scott Fitzgerald, Ezra Pound, Ford Madox Ford…recognize any of those names?

I've always had a special relationship with bookstores and libraries – this is one that won't be forgotten!

A Letter from My Second Born

This letter was an email format greeting to me. From my son Allen. He says he sent his thoughts to humor me and make me laugh. He accomplished both those goals. In the context of these words he also reflects his goodness to me without realizing he has done so. My son has worked diligently throughout his life to save for his future. He has achieved tremendous success in everything he has ever set out to accomplish. These years of effort have always reflected humility and a desire to help others. My heart fills with pride each time I see the qualities his father and I dreamed about and hoped to instill within him.

Near Derby time in Louisville

Was up early this morning cleaning bathrooms and making a trip to Home Depot. And, to my tasty pleasure, diving into a plate of eggs on toast at my favorite greasy all night diner. Life unfolds at places like that and the real people tend to hang out there -half homeless and many less than working class. It's the kind of place Jesus would stop on a cross state walk to take a disciple fishing on Kentucky Lake. I doubt you'd find Him at the Derby Saturday.

Guess I never really understood until this morning my brother's attraction to more than off the trail places. Made me chuckle at the endless parade of those caught up in the pomp and circumstance of desired perceptions. Then again, my Lexus looked very new in the parking lot despite the

171,000 miles. The only part of me that fit 'in' was my Carmargo fishing hat. With thousands of miles under the brim, it's felt the power of the Kenai River, the salt of the Caribbean Sea and the warmth of a sunrise over the Gulf of Mexico. Then even again, it's a hat that sports the logo of an exclusive club that has even turned away billionaire members of the community from joining. Damn, I'm down to my underwear now and they're even a name brand.

Well…. glancing at my Rolex, I recognize that it's 6:10 a.m. and Home Depot opened 10 minutes ago. To hell with my Allen Edmonds, they'll have to get wet in the rain. Brand new pair. Should have never left my Ben Silver umbrella in the car. At least the shoes were factory seconds and I paid thirty-five cents on the dollar. They'll have to get wet. Didn't stop to recognize the continuing rain while I grabbed them to wear. Of course they, like my other 15 pairs of shoes, reside in the hall closet so dirt won't be tracked on my new gazillion dollar a square foot carpet, no doubt, name brand.

Guess the point of this is to encourage myself to further skip the societal Kool Aid people guzzle by the gallon. It's laced with the Jim Jones special additive, whether or not recognized. And just maybe, the observations of my morning will inspire a belly laugh from you that will wake the owls on the other side of the lake.

Blessed Harmony

This autumn day began and ends in blessed tenderness.

Morning fog enveloped my senses while I drank of pungent coffee and memories.

So adored was I ....so long adored in the valleys and upon the mountaintops of living. Always a heart and an ear to hear me.

Eyes and lips to smile at my exuberance.

Blowing the scarlet and purple leaves of season gave the consuming fragrance of lemon balm to my longing senses. Mulching brought the sweet aroma of artimesia.

Clothes on the line for feeling the sunshine.

Grass surrounding the aged persimmon tree, bright green and delicious to smell. Morning Glories are flaunting their last, soon awaiting the bite of frost. Frost white and glimmering early morning October. The lake, this water - often the color of hammered pewter, I never tire of looking upon, reflects the brilliance of brave standing trees.

Ending of day. Candles lit to soften the coming of dusk. Music playing to chase away the melancholy of knowing there is no one here to share these feeling with just now.

And so…. my heart overflowing with the blessed tenderness of it all, I'll share with you.

October 20, 2003

Colorado Ride

As I began to plan our wedding day after my prince had proposed and we had set a date, there was no question of which friend I would choose to be my maid of honor. My dear Sheila, whom I'd met in a Field Biology class in my second year of college. She'd been here in our town for several years and each of us 'knew of' the other. She told me she always thought I'd be way too 'uppity' for her, until the day she saw me sitting barefoot on the floor of the science building restroom, calmly enjoying a cigarette. A bond of friendship began then that continues now and many sweet memories flood my mind as I write this story.

We always stayed in contact with each other through long letters and she had phoned several times during the last dark days of my husband's life. Through that hot June and July time, I often daydreamed of being in the Rocky Mountains. Those daydreams helped me cope with my lack of sleep, my fears, the horrible dread losing him and kept me from crying.

Just a week after the memorial service for the Prince, Sheila called to invite me to Colorado. Her younger sister Jennifer had kept the guest register at my wedding reception, so there had always been an emotional connection even to 'little sister' Jen. The two of them planned to have me join them on a sister trip that they had already planned. They decided that inviting me to join them would be a good grief gift. This invitation and thought of me was incredibly unique and exactly what I needed after the years of fear and loss of sleep I'd endured during Raphael's sickness.

Jen, who lives here, picked me up on her way to the airport in Nashville. That first night in Parker, Colorado, at Sheila's house, sleeping with the windows open to the cool mountain air, I knew it was only the beginning of a grand adventure.

We drove off the next morning, eager to begin our escapade. Jen had planned the trip completely and judiciously. Each place we visited or spent a night was a delicious surprise to me but ever so carefully chosen by Jen. Two nights in Durango at an old refurbished hotel and a steam train ride to Silverton, a little town 9,000 feet in elevation. Afterward we drove high into the mountains to a dude ranch, for a horseback riding experience. They were so excited about these plans, but not me! My back had begun to ache the night before. Years of overeating had left me heavy and out of shape. They had ridden horses growing up; I hadn't been on one since I was a child. The night before we had purchased matching shirts and Aussie hats for the two day ride. We laughed as we were driving in the gate saying we hoped our guide was a handsome cowboy. Much to our chagrin, he arrived skinny- bone skinny- and his face had wrinkles upon wrinkles. When he smiled, teeth were missing. We giggled and exchanged 'looks' with each other, concluding that Barry definitely was not a dream cowboy. He began to patiently explain in his western 'twang' that the horses were old Appaloosas and very gentle. I looked back at the beautiful A- framed cottage and mentioned that I'd much rather stay behind and spend the night there. Oh my! It looked so inviting and comfortable. 'Oh no', said Barry, ' Honey you're gonna love this high ride up the mountain! 'Why, gal, the spot I've picked out to stop for lunch is so high you can see four states from the place!" I explained that my back was aching and perhaps this wasn't the time to be on a horse. 'Oh naw', he said, 'horse back riding is the very medicine for an aching back, don't ya know?' It took a while to make certain we three were in the saddle and had our tepid bottle of water hung to the side. It wasn't long until we began to climb higher and higher and the view was spectacular. My horse seemed sure-footed and easy to control and I began to relax and enjoy the ride. Barry turned his head and yelled, 'Don't let them horses eat that weed they keep a trying to get to!' Jennifer, bravest of us all, asked why. 'Wellll, let me put it this away gals, it makes them , uh….gassy!' Barry replied. We asked him if he had any way of contacting the ranch in case we had problems and he said, 'Heck no, we don't need no help, we're just fine the way we are!' 'And gals, you keep a lookin down at them there mushrooms, don't pick any I say, don't even touch them darned things!' Again, Jennifer the brave one, asked why. 'Let's just say they'll make you crazy in the head, that's why'.

We had ridden several miles and stopped in a high meadow to take pictures, when Barry told us we would very soon be riding into an area called 'Bear Claw Pass'. 'Now gals', he said, 'there's them big Aspen trees a growing there and you can see the scratches of them bear claws all over them trees.'

'These here horses may spook if a bear or mountain lion's been around recent like.' If your horse spooks and begins to run, hold on tight to that there saddle horn and don't let im buck you off, you hear?' We heard and mentally filed away, 'hold tight to saddle horn, and don't let him buck you off.'

Bear Claw Pass was indeed a glorious place with hundreds of huge Aspen trees growing all around. The ones with the largest trunks all bore the wounds of scratching bear claws. We had just ridden out of the Aspen forest when our horses began to whinny and took off charging forward at a very fast gallop. Everyone else's horse ran to my left but my old Appaloosa ran right, fairly flying for an aged one and expelling gas like crazy! I hung on to the saddle horn and prayed! He ran between two huge Aspen trees and in just a moment I realized that every part of the horse and I had cleared the close distance - except my right knee. I heard a 'whap' when knee encountered the tree. I felt no pain but realized an immediate swelling and tingling sensation. I yelled, 'Barry, I hurt my knee!' He leaned back from his horse and asked, 'Are you a bleedin?' Well...I wasn't a bleedin and felt no pain in the knee, so I decided I must be brave and keep on riding.

An hour or so later we reached the breath taking high point and stopped for lunch. When I put weight on my right foot, I still didn't feel any pain, even though my knee had by now swollen to the size of a large cantaloupe. We peacefully ate our pitiful lunch of a thin slice of roast beef and butter on white bread. We had only our tepid water from the canteens, to drink. It began to thunder, then lightening knifed across the vivid blue sky.

'Uh oh,' Barry exclaimed, 'better get you gals to cover, looks like there's gonna be a storm.' We were simply marveling at nature's grand showing of beauty and were reluctant to move. Just then a huge clap of thunder shook the mountainside and I tried to stand up. Thankfully, Shelia was there to support my body. That's when Barry happened to look around and see my swollen knee. 'Oh mercy sakes alive Georgia! Why didn't you tell me that knee was that bad?' The only thing I could think of in reply was, 'I don't know.' Then he began barking orders to Sheila and Jennifer, 'you gals get Georgia down by that crick there and take her britches off and put some of that there cold mud on her knee, I'm a ridin back to the ranch for help.' He put our horses into a make shift corral nearby, gave us the smelly old rain slickers for cover and jumped on his horse. Jennifer yelled, 'Barry wait, didn't you say you had a gun with you?' 'Ah…yep I did', he said. Jennifer said, 'why don't you leave it with us for protection while you are gone?' 'Uh…nope, can't do that', he replied. And Jennifer ever the brave one said, 'Why not? We might need it.' He turned ever so slowly and said, 'Can't do that gal, y'all might shoot Georgia!' Off he rode at a fast gallop. I told the girls that I wasn't going to take my pants off out there in the middle of nowhere for anybody. They could just put the cold, wet mud over my brand new jeans! They settled me down with a small log for my head and one for my leg. Jennifer had just gotten the rain slickers over our bodies when it truly began to rain. Sheila seemed to enjoy placing the mud on my knee. I told them I was so glad there weren't any insects around, as I was an 'insect target' lying on the bare ground. After Jen took our picture, I settled my hat over my face. I said, 'Girls, this is what the cowboys do in the movies.' The hat didn't stay there long because we began to tell stories and giggle. I looked up and said, 'Girls, those two big contorted Aspen trees look like they are making love.' That brought gales of laughter again. It wasn't long until we heard the four-wheel drive truck coming up the mountain. There were no roads there so that had to bring in something that could take the terrain. Barry said later we beat all he'd ever seen, three gals out there in the wilderness, a thousand miles from home with one injured, and we were laughing! Out of the truck came a handsome man – at least I thought he was handsome – and Barry introduced him as 'Indian Joe'. He helped me into the truck and drove me to the lodge. When we arrived at the office he said, 'Now honey, you've been sittin' awfully close to me, guess I'd best move you over fore anybody gets any ideas.'

He checked me into the little A-frame lodge that I had seen before we left. He asked if I was hungry and I said, 'yes, I'm starved!' Then he asked, 'Honey Gal, are you in pain?' I assured him that I wasn't and that I had some over- the-counter pain medication with me. While he went to get my supper, I took a hot shower and changed into clean clothes and propped myself up in the soft, fluffy bed. Indian Joe returned with a delicious meal and an ice bag for my knee. He explained that he would be leaving and there would be no one around until morning. He said, 'You poor dear child, your husband has just died and now you are far from home and hurt!' I told him I had found a coffee pot, a good supply of coffee and had my journal and books with me. I assured him I would say a prayer and be totally fine. He told me he would be back in the morning to take my order for breakfast, leaned over and kissed the top of my head and closed the door behind him.

I spent a peaceful night, reading, writing in my journal and praying. I began thinking about Sheila and Jennifer, my two dear friends and I decided that long ago God had put us together and that was why we share such comfort and goodness. I realized when I dated my journal that it was exactly one month since my prince's birthday- his last one here on earth with me, and then I let the tears flow until I felt a sense of peace and finally drifted to sleep.

Next morning I perked coffee just in time for Joe's arrival with my breakfast. I profusely thanked him and asked what I could do to repay his kindness. He said, ' Honey, you're from Kentucky, right?' I said, 'Yes'. He said, 'I'm only half Indian. My momma was from Kentucky and could bake the best Chess pies in the world!' 'Do you bake Chess pies and could I have the recipe?' I assured him I would send him more than one recipe and gave him a good-bye hug.

An hour or so later the girls came struggling into the door, hungry, wet, dirty and worn to a frazzle. I said, 'Welcome to my hot shower, now tell me all about your night.' We laughed and laughed when they told of having to take a shovel when they went to pee and having to make their own teepee to crawl into before going to sleep.

We left the ranch and drove back into Durango to a doctor. He told me I had wonderful knees and nothing was broken. He instructed me to just wrap the knee and continue on our vacation. The girls were so loving and concerned about me, that is for a while. They stopped at a drug store and got a cold wrap for my knee and settled me into the back of the car. I was pampered constantly until we went shopping in Santa Fe; I had to sit upright to make room for their treasures in the back seat. Even the trunk was full! Jennifer loved telling about my bruises to everyone. She thought I was such a lovely purple, green, black and blue - from my private parts right down to my ankle. She would fall into gales of laughter every time I undressed in the motel room. I knew it was just her sweet sense of humor. She requested a wheelchair and patiently pushed me around the Georgia O'Keefe museum. She even asked for a wheelchair in the Denver airport and we were ushered right on to the plane!

Boys always told me I had beautiful legs when I was a teen, I suppose that means I have good strong knees too. One thing I do know, I have angels for friends!

My House By The Side of The Road
A Place for My Heart

Memories of my parents searching for just the right place for a home when I was only six years old, surface within my mind often. They had rented from before my birth and taken in our grandparents when they lost the farm to debts they couldn't pay. Much emotion went into the choosing of that house and moving day was one of excitement and joy. It proved to be a wonderful place to grow… a cattle barn for Dad's business, an orchard and garden spot and a large lawn with dappled shade. From the age of six until I left home after college at twenty-one, I slept in the same bedroom which faced the morning sun.

When I married my Prince, I had no way of knowing just how many times we would be uprooted. We moved many times and most all of them in the Midwest where his profession took him. I remember being so full of joy when we were being transferred to Tennessee. Finally! I thought, close to home. That is until I looked at a map and realized we were moving the distant eastern part of the state, to a little mountain town. Almost three hundred miles from Western Kentucky and twice a world away from all that I had known growing up. The mountains and the people were akin to fiction stories I had read in the past. So foreign this land to me; visits home were a balm to my soul.

It seemed like forever, that we were living in apartments and rental houses in one state or another. Always the mandate to ever-changing locations. And when the company finally told us we would be in one place, at least for a longer period of time, it was miles from anything I had ever known. North East Iowa meant long, snowy winters and people with names and ways that were so foreign to my southern heritage. In the days of few interstate highways, a trip home took thirteen hours of two -lane driving. Of course there were experiences of joy, as our second son's birth while we were renting a farmhouse called Bonny View. The lilac harbor and garden spot were beautiful and the taste of my first rhubarb like no other I've ever known. Possibly because the glacial soil is black as jet and abundantly rich.

Always at the mercy of the job that kept a roof over our heads, I quietly endured an aching heart. I did it for love, the grand love of the man to whom I had promised my all.

In my mind and romantic imaginings, there was a little house by the side of the road. A place where I could have all my mementoes of passion… pictures, china, crystal and lace. Carpet, walls and rooms in colors of soft pastel painted and placed there by me, lovingly reflecting my personality. During this time I was drawn to purchase a print that illustrated a stream of pale blue, trees of gentlest green and skies of wonderful pastels. At the time I didn't really know why it soothed me so very much. When troubled or lonely, I looked at it in a meditative way. Looking back, I see that the print was a semblance of my 'little house' vision.

One day while visiting Mom and Dad in West Kentucky, home and place of soft southernisms, I found the house and it's surrounding that I had dreamed about in fantasy. It began as a leisurely drive to see the area where Dad had ranged cattle when I was only a wee girl. Daddy wanted to surprise me with the immense changes of the area. The Tennessee Valley Authority had sold this land, on the banks of the Blood River access of the lake, to private ownership; and the once unscathed, wooded pastureland waterfront, was now home to a new housing subdivision! As Daddy was driving and I was exclaiming, we turned onto a street that followed a peninsula and there inside the circled street was a patch of land containing two houses. It was almost like the scene from 'Miracle on Thirty Forth Street' when I looked to see a little house all grown up and neglected. A ' For Sale' sign on the edge of the weedy lawn let me know I could go look inside the house.

Mind you, it sat so pitiful among all other beautiful large and well-tended homes. When Daddy stopped the car at my request, I ran up and looked into a large window to see a little kitchen with a fireplace. Well into the afternoon and next day I could not get that little house out of my mind. When the Prince called that night I told him about finding the place and the fact that it was for sale. Now we were in the middle of renovating our large house in Iowa and I knew he probably would dismiss my excitement, as he was often prone to do. He said, 'when I come we'll drive out and look at that little place.' I told him it just spoke to my heart.

When he came to take us back to Iowa and stark realities, we called the realtor and looked once again at the place. Next day he told me we must go to town on business. I had no idea just what business he was referring to, but dutifully rode along.

There at the courthouse was a deed already prepared in my name only. When I overcame my astonishment I asked, 'Why? My Prince responded, 'It's for you, a place for some day dreaming my sweet.'

Finally that day came and he began with hammer and nails to cover my little house with the cedar shingles I had dreamed of, in a long ago moment of whimsy.

In only a brief span of peaceful time, working together to change the house became long days of joy and labor. We worked and played together, having a picnic lunch on top the roof he was shingling, made decisions about where new windows would go, and often kissed after a walk to 'look back' upon our progress from the lakeshore.

All too briefly I came to know that the most dreaded of nightmares could come true.

Death took him away.

Our first-born son worked hard to comfort me and keep his last promises to his father, dutifully following his plans.

After a little passage of time, we departed the Prince's frugal ways and began to make it totally mine.

The setting sun of afternoon beckons to me through windows I have chosen. Placed just so, the moon in certain seasons, shines down upon my bed. The sun touches the lace curtains brought from Germany, my heritage country and given in love by a friend. It sparkles upon the circles of glass that hold them back —circles of glass that captured my imagination one bright October day while enjoying a Central Illinois craft fair with friend Ginny. She said, 'Now tell me, just what are you going to do with those?' I did not know then, but now they reflect a part of me. The sun lights the brilliance of crystal and wheel cut glass given to my mother by Aunt Georgia Lee so long ago in an act of thankfulness.

It bounces and flames around the mirrored shelves of the golden colored cabinet my mother, a depression child, bought in a moment of delight.

As it touches the brown tiles of the flooring, I hurry out to gaze at the afternoon west... lovely in lavender, coral and azure. Only a dream for many years, now I am surrounded by the once – coveted pastel serenity of my print.

I call to dear friends next door, 'Oh come and feel the afternoon gift that turns the trees growing upon the banks of the lake to gold!' And I praise God for the vision of water so clear, reflecting a Great Blue Heron in flight; I listen to the serenade of birdsongs, Wrens, Cardinals, Mocking Birds and Woodpeckers. And sometimes at night I hear a Whippoorwill call and bullfrogs singing their deep voiced songs, from the edge of the lake.

Images of my Prince look out at me from carefully chosen frames. Strangers come and go with compliments upon the garden, where depending upon the season, Hollyhocks grow in grand profusion and Ivy and Clematis trail on the fence.

Mother's yellow and purple Iris bloom alongside the Snow Drops that grew in my childhood yard. Shrubs of Rosemary abound to brush against, Lemon Balm, Mint, Savory and Thyme are there for the pleasure of my taking. I'm filled with joy and pride of my labors when others comment upon the serene beauty of this dear place.

Here am I, having endured a shattered heart and surfaced to find love again. Loving deeply a man from my long ago past…a man of phenomenal strength and beauty. God has given to me, the gift of realizing that as well as nightmares, dreams do come true. Mine is a life fulfilled…two blessed sons of great character, a wise and fine man to love and be loved, friends in abundance, and God's safekeeping.

I whisper a prayer, while wrapped in peace, love and thanksgiving within this house by the side of the road.

Early Winter Evenings

Early winter evenings are a cozy thing. They give me a time for introspective thoughts. As I say in poetry, it's the time 'when darkness comes early and dawn comes late.' Most of the thirty-five years of my married life were spent in the Midwest where winters are long. Before my dear husband succumbed to a cruel illness, he moved me back to my childhood home in Western Kentucky. Winters here are just long enough for a resting time. They come subtly in soft stages, not crashing down like they do in Iowa and Wisconsin. By early March daffodils are blooming in crisp springtime glory.

One evening recently, my cousin called to ask for my help with an assignment her son needed to complete for school. I said 'yes' gladly, as it has been a joy to help him. This time the request was an interview of a person over the age of sixty. Email made the task easy. And, the experience was surprisingly delightful. Answering the questions moved me back in space to a wonderful period of living. The topic was my teenage years. Following are the questions and my answers.

Question:
Where did you live?

Answer:
I lived here in Murray, Kentucky where I was born in 1939.

What was school like? Favorite teachers? I attended a very special school on the campus of Murray State University. It was built in 1927 and first called the Laboratory School, later the Training School and finally, University School. It was a school for training prospective teachers. In addition to having a major teacher, we had several new student teachers each semester. We received a unique education as we were part of the university and used all the facilities on campus. We were watching Shakespearean plays by the time we were in the upper grades. We were required to learn to swim before we could graduate high school. All of our teachers were also on faculty at the college. My favorite ones were… our music teacher who taught all twelve grades, instrumental and voice. He was Josiah Darnall, a wonderful man; Miss Lottie Suiter was our fifth grade teacher and instilled in me the love of poetry and appreciation of literature. She also taught my college literature course years later; Mrs. Lillian Lowery was another favorite of mine. We were among the first high school students in the nation to have a course in psychology. Teaching that course was her idea and it took some effort on her part to convince the administration to allow that subject to be taught to high school seniors. She also taught English, Speech and Drama. One year she took sabbatical and lived in Japan. Lois Sparks filled her position and took a few of us to State in dramatics. Her husband became the president of the university after I had graduated college and married. They were loving, motivated people who truly believed in education.

Question:
What jobs did you have?

Answer:
Our school had a Junior Store on the third floor of the building. When we became juniors, we could work in the store, however, our labor there was a learning experience without pay.

In the summer I sold watermelons from our front yard. My dad said it would teach me many lessons. How to weigh produce, figure price per pound and get to know people. It did all those things. I also worked at the local theatre when I became sixteen. I was one of many ushers. We wore uniforms and showed people to their seats with a flashlight. Just before movie time we went back stage and pulled a large rope, moving the velvet curtain back to expose the screen. I made fifteen cents an hour. I also worked in my mother's restaurant, but never enjoyed that job. I just wasn't 'cut out' to be a waitress!

Question:
Describe your relationships with parents and peers and talk about dating.

Answer:
I had a wonderful relationship with my parents. I think our grandparents helped that situation. I did have a tendency toward rebellion that my brother did not share. I realize now that our personalities differed in that way. My grandfather died when I was seven years old but grandmother lived to see me graduate from college. She lived in a little house next door that Daddy had built for her. I spent a lot of time with her. Mom and Dad called it 'helping to take care of her', but the taking care went both ways. So many lessons learned from my hours with her.

We played Rook at the dining table in the winter and croquet on the lawn in the summer. Mom and Dad took us to drive- in movies and to visit relatives. Once a year mother closed her business and we drove to Texas to spend two weeks with aunts, uncles and cousins. Mother also took us often to visit older relatives who lived in the area. She was grand at showing them attention and love. I learned so very much from all of them.

I had boyfriends who rode their bicycles to my house to spend time sitting on the front porch. Dating was such an innocent thing. One girlfriend lived in the country and her dad took us frog gigging on warm summer nights. Small groups of boys and girls. I think it was his way of keeping us out of trouble.

When driving entered our lives we did a lot of cruising. Gas was all of fifteen cents a gallon. Church dates were popular and approved by all parents.

Our school didn't have a football team but the city high school did and I dated boys who played and went to after- game dances and programs at their school. Both schools performed plays and musicals several times a year.

Question:
What types of things did you do for entertainment?

Answer:
Entertainment was church, school events, gospel singings, birthday parties, movies and parties at friends' houses. The roller rink was a popular place for some, but forbidden to me as I suffered night leg aches and my parents thought skating might make it worse. Truth be told, it may have helped the situation but I was never to know.

Question:
What type of clothing did you wear and what was popular?

Answer:
Clothing was very distinctive with three colors being prominent: lavender and, pink and black for both boys and girls. Yes, pink for the guys too. They wore classic dress shirts with button down collars and we girls wore them too. Lavender and black was another combination to help a teen feel they were 'in' style. Full skirts and crisply starched and ironed cotton blouses for spring and summer for we girls. We even ironed the tops and shorts of our gym uniforms. We wore sweaters and wool straight skirts, and full felt skirts for winter. Boys wore button down the front dress shirts, some with big collars they could flip up in back. Dress pants were often worn, but jeans were beginning to be the rage. What we termed 'pegged pants' were jeans taken in at the bottom to achieve a slender appearance. The movie star James Dean had a great affect on the male fashion of the time. A single string of fake pearls for church and dressy occasions were a must for we girls. The only make up we dared to wear was sometimes a pale pink lipstick, purchased at the Five and Dime store and called 'Pink Queen'. Shoes were same for boys and girls- penny loafers and saddle oxfords. A penny was worn in the slit in front of the loafers and saddle oxfords were black and white or brown and white. Only our shoes for gym class differed greatly from boys to girls. We dressed in our very best for church and special school events.

Sports coats were a must for the boys and they all wanted a white one. The pink carnation was the flower for our time.

Question:
What type of music was popular? What musical artists?

Answer:
Music was experiencing a revolution during my teen years. We broke away from our parents' big band music and danced and sang the songs of our time. Most were romantic and we remember the words even now. Elvis Presley debuted in 1955, the year I was sixteen. My friend Gayle, who lived in Memphis, knew him. I often rode down to Memphis on the Greyhound bus to visit her. One night at a downtown movie house, Elvis came for a private showing. We were standing on the sidewalk waiting for him. As he came walking by us he tripped and fell into me. I could not utter a sound as he gently kissed me first on one cheek and then another, all the time apologizing to me!

Before Elvis, Carl Perkins recording, 'Blue Suede Shoes' was a huge hit and a good swing dancing song. ' Rock Around The Clock,' 'Hey There' by Rosemary Clooney, 'Happy, Happy Birthday Baby,' ' For Your Precious Love' 'A White Sports Coat' and 'Sincerely' were a few among the many. The Platters, The Temptations, Ray Charles, Peggy Lee and Little Richard are just small examples of the many stars of our time.

Beyond music, I had a great love for literature. I was an avid reader from the time I learned to read. The School library kept me entertained with a wealth of choices. Our English teacher required book reports and I read so many authors. Some I remember are, Jane Austin, John Steinbeck, Faulkner, and of course Bronte's Wuthering Heights.

My classmates who read this will silently, (or loudly) add song titles, artists, authors, books and details that I have forgotten, and I'll love them for remembering the things I have forgotten.

And now, through my story you the reader have experienced a little mind trip through a portion of "The Fabulous Fifties.

Unbridled Tenderness

My own private definition of unbridled tenderness:

'Those moments when joy and emotions completely overcome one's senses'

Spring moved me to pot and plant, as always. This year I lovingly placed a start of creeping thyme in an old metal container. Found in the garage, it was stored for possibilities. Returning home from a brief away time, as I always do, walked around checking every growing thing in my garden of solitude. The old bucket had become an overflowing vessel for tiny, aromatic thyme, covered with minute pale pink blossoms. The finding moved my heart to tears of joy. And then laughter as I thought perhaps my neighbors, should they over hear, would conclude once again.... she, is one eccentric woman! Oh the experiences that have molded me to this sensitivity! Surrendering many dearly loved ones in such a short span of time, watching the love of my life, my Prince slowly die away, enduring times of intense pain. Living along with my children through heart rendering disappointments, physical and mental agony. Being visited by that cold, hard fear for them, and the all too cold reality of helplessness. Wanting with all of my being to change it, to endure it for them, and knowing I cannot.

My friend Paula refers to these moments of unbridled joy as 'attacks of deliciousness', and I do like that terminology, but I've chosen my own to go along with hers. As we grow older it is guaranteed that we will have endured pain and loss. In poetry I say, 'it's what living will surely do.' Growing through adversity teaches us to appreciate simple experiences with intense joy, if we only let go and allow ourselves to do so. Joy that those of youth cannot understand. Truthfully, I accept it with deep gratitude. Having always been a romantic by nature, my tender being has magnified with living.

Falling in love, when I never expected to ever love this deeply again in my lifetime, has added such feelings of exuberance to every single moment. Sunrise, sunset, moon stages, tiny creatures, friendships, dancing, singing, planting and all the very simple aspects of daily living have taken on a newness.

As a new bride, I marveled at the love I felt for my prince and the dream come true days and nights together. I found a poem in a Lady's Home Journal magazine, saving it in our wedding book. And it is there today. It so described my wonder.

Rewards

'I never looked for roses, just for thorns,
To feel a little smoother to the touch,
And now at last a rose my heart adorns
To take away the sting of thorns and such.

I never looked for music, just for chords
To sound a little softer to the ear,
And now my soul enjoys it's own rewards –
Enchanted melodies I seem to hear.

I never looked for rapture, just for peace
To brush away the tears I could not share.
And then upon the wings of swift release,
I found these lovely things – for you were there.
Jessyca Russell Gaver

This beautiful poem went with us each time he was hospitalized, placed by the bed in a little frame. The wonder never lessened, only increased for the thirty five years we were married. I asked that this poem, along with mine, be read at his memorial.

A few years later I wrote a poem that appears in my first book.

Where Love Lies

In the late of September
I chose a puddle of sunlight,
Lifted up my face to feel the warmth
Upon eyelids, just above that place
Where love lies.

Just days ago -or so it seems,
I found cool shade, soft breeze
To lift away drops of sweat
Between my breasts upon that place
Where love lies.

Just days ago – or so it seems
Daffodils bloomed in the cool of spring.
I longed for hands to tenderly touch
My back in gentleness, upon that place
Where love lies.

Just days ago – or so it seems,
In the cold crisp air that winter brings,
I longed for arms around me strong,
To hold, to surround that place
Where love lies.

Just days ago – or so it seems,
These things of hope
These things of dreams
Were there

And in the light of September sun
I weep from sound of violin
And long for a gentle kiss, a caress…. upon that place
Where love lies.

Little did I know that in a few short months, that longing would be
answered, and I would fall in love again. Differently, deeply, sweetly and
completely.

Color Love
In spirit I go to the bible I keep
And reverently seek
To
Color love

For this grand emotion
I cannot speak with mortal

Voice

With all devotion
I borrow, 'tongues of angels'
Those I often entreat to watch over my loves

'love is patient, love is kind…rejoices in the truth…always protects,
always trusts,
always hopes, always perseveres, love never fails.' 1 Corinthians 13:4-8

In mind I reach for a rainbow
Color love so
Grandly
A
Rainbow

Hot, sultry summer has come to my little corner of the world. Far
Western Kentucky, nestled within a lush green geography, surrounded
by rivers and lakes. I am in the candle light time of life. Just a few days

ago, the ringing phone brought tears of regret and sorrow. Another friend has died. We met in high school, this slight of form, tall young man. This week I stood in the country cemetery, surrounded by heat of summer sun and friends, waiting the moments when the preacher would 'talk Craig's soul to rest'. In memory I returned to the Christmas I came home from California, dressed in expensive clothes and showing off classy make up, long dangling earrings and a strawberry blonde hairstyle. Talking 'California' seemed to mortify my mother. I found it amusing to be adult, independent and able to mortify her.

An invitation call came from friend Craig, who was a senior in college that year, for a party. His parents were away and he desired my presence for a night of fun. Candles were lit among the holiday decorations. Champagne and caviar served upon fine china dishes and delicate crystal glasses. A group of his newly acquired college friends filled the room. I laughed and told him I was so impressed! I never knew how far away from this little Kentucky town Craig must have shopped for these sophistications. From his long arms around me he said, ' I had to pull out all the stops to impress you, after all, you live in California now!'

Perhaps to some, this entreating to immerse one's self in the blessings of each night and each day may seem redundant. However, not even with a shed of reluctance, will I admit or regret my passion! Strains of dramatic music impel me to dance glorious tango, waltzing lightly around the hardwood floor upon the arms of a charming man, invigorates my very soul. For every precious moment I alight the ' winged and grand horse of living' and move every so swiftly along... unbridled in fresh amazement!

Earth Your Dancing Place

Beneath heaven's vault
Remember always walking
Through halls of cloud
Down aisles of sunlight
Or through high hedges
Of the green rain
Walk in the world
High heeled with swirl of cape
Hand at the sword hilt
Of your pride
Keep a tall throat
Remain aghast at life

Enter each day
As upon a stage
Lighted and waiting
For your step
Crave upward as flame
Have keenness in the nostril
Give your eyes
To agony or rapture

Train you hands
As birds to be.

Anonymous author

The Waltz of Awakening

Some two years after the loss of my prince, I had begun to 'awaken' from the long darkness of loss and tears. Mornings were often a gifting of glorious sunrises and deep breaths of blessings.

Recognizing my grief, a dear younger friend from school days called to invite me to a dance party. I politely declined, telling her that moving with grace just wasn't a talent of mine. Beautiful Judy would not take my excuses and insisted I come and allow it to be a part of moving on with living. She is such an intuitive person and realized the need for me to be with people once again. I had virtually cloistered myself at home for months on end.

Our reunion from high school days began when she and I met town one day and I invited her home for lunch and a girlfriend visit. We relived our long ago friendship and I told her stories of the childhood days when her husband Don's parents and mine were dear friends. Upon her persistence, I agreed to attend the dance party with she and Don. I did look forward with anticipation remembering childhood days with Don.

That evening was the beginning of a 'bursting forth' for me. Meeting many warm, gracious people who could dance so fantastically, made me want to try. What a delight meeting Lyda and Dick, Sara and Terry, reuniting with Elsie and Charles – 'Boogie' – Thurman. Getting to know dear, sweet Joan, Jimmy and Doris, and realizing that my Dana friend was among those who had learned to ballroom dance, inspired me to do more than just dream of waltzing.

As I began to spend many pleasant hours with Don and Judy, I realized that they had become a magnification of those dear young people from my hometown. I often tell others about them and say that they each will have a 'star in their crown' for the goodness and love they have shown to me, not to mention their kindnesses to so many people. Bringing me into their circle of dance friends opened a new world for me.

In poetry I thank all my dance friends for taking in a widow and making her feel like a queen. These days, not only do my feet waltz, tango and swing, but my heart does as well!

This sad caterpillar burst forth from the binding of a dark chrysalis, to become a floating, dancing butterfly, blessed with the ability to 'take to the dance floor' in company with the grandest of friends! They truly inspired my 'Waltz of Awakening'.

"ON WITH THE DANCE, LET THE JOY BE UNCONFINED."
- Lord Byron

God's Child
Fingers of Flame

Absolutely nothing that I write explaining my rise from grievous 'ashes of loss' would be complete without my humble tribute to a priceless friendship – that of my friend John.

This bond of respect and love began with John's father, Josiah, whom I came to know at the tender age of eight. Josiah was our music teacher at that grand laboratory school on the campus of the college here in Murray. He profoundly affected my life, as well as each and every child he taught.

All of his students knew his family, wife Lucinda and sons, John and Robert.

John was nearer in age to my class, so therefore, I knew him better than his younger brother.

I found John again quiet by accident and many years after our time at the laboratory school. The finding was a truly wonderful kind of circumstance. While at a dear friend's house for a Christmas party, I heard music playing that touched my heart. After inquiring about where she bought this compact disc, I went the very next day and bought a copy of both 'Light Jazz for Christmas Eve' and ' Light Jazz for Christmas.'

When I opened the CD and read the inside information, to my delight, I discovered it was arranged and performed by Josiah's son, John. My soul swelled with pride for him. I sat down and wrote a letter, mailing it to the post office address listed on the CD's insert. When John received it, Josiah was in the hospital, recovering from the first of many complications.

Finding Josiah and Lucinda after my 'awakening' time from grief was such a joy. The timing was almost too late, as Josiah's health had rapidly deteriorated in a short span of time. We lost that grand man to God's arms, soon after I had dedicated my second book to him. I gently gave him up to Heaven, rather than have him suffer a long period of this life on Earth.

After Josiah's death, John took his father's place within my heart's admiration. Being closer to my age than his father and sharing more commonalities, my admiration and friendship for John grows stronger and becomes more priceless as we continue this journey of life.

John loves coming to Western Kentucky to relive memories of his childhood and to escape the confines of professional life in Nashville.

He has received several gold records for his special projects of the past. His instrument of choice is guitar and, as I say in poetry, as he plays, 'his finger tips, a candle flame of fire'. His work is primarily instrumental and he tells me that people who listen write to tell him that they literally feel God's power within his creations.'

And, Oh! He can be so much fun when relaxing to play. I love riding in one of his many awesome cars, exploring the back roads of Calloway County, or in town searching out friends from our past. And when he relaxes in my home and plays a guitar solo and sings, just for me, while sitting in the kitchen sharing a cup of hot tea, or when we sit on the porch and watch the lake and sky, I have, if for only a few hours, that private joy of having him just to myself!

This friendship of ours continues to bless my heart with ever- flowing love and admiration.

"There are persons so radiant, so genial, so kind, so pleasure-bearing, that you instinctively feel in their presence they do you good; whose coming into a room is like the bringing of a lamp there." ---Henry Ward Beecker

Bouffant Daddy's

My dear friend Lyda from dancing called one day, just to talk and unburden her soul. She told me of an upcoming trip to St. Louis to attend a conference for her business. I mentioned that I too would be making a trip that direction as a nephew was getting married in a little town near there. She asked if I would like to join her and her manager and spend the week in the Ritz Carlton Hotel with them. My heavens that sounded like fun. After a phone call to a friend who lived there, asking him if he could transport me to and from the hotel to the wedding, I called dear blond and blue-eyed Lyda to accept the invitation for the trip.

The morning we left home, rain was pouring down and wind was blowing strongly against the car. The weather did not affect the 'girly' conversations inside where we were warm and dry. I had agreed to navigate the St. Louis area because I knew the city and surroundings well, having lived there on two different occasions.

Lyda mentioned that before checking into the hotel, we had to make a stop at a beauty shop. She had met a man while at a dancing competition earlier in the month and made an appointment to get a very special haircut from him. After all, any cosmetologist who did hair for ballroom competitions, had to be among the best at their business. I asked for the location of the shop and she said, 'Here it is, I found it on the Internet'. One look at the print out and I said, 'Oh we can't go there!!!' 'But we HAVE to go there' she said. I said, 'Lyda, that's in the middle of East St.

Louis and in a high crime area, we cannot go there!' It was at this point in this animated conversation that I had the presence of mind to ask the name of the shop. 'It's called Bouffant Daddy's', she proudly exclaimed. Now I have to tell you that even though I had not known her long, I had concluded that 'naive' or even 'sheltered' should have been her middle name. So, I asked to borrow her cell phone to call the number on the paper she handed me, thinking I'll ask directions and then cancel this crazy appointment. When I called, I was relieved to find out that the shop was in an upscale area just outside of the city and that the Internet directions were incorrect.

'Well my dear,' I said, 'warm up your credit card and take the very next exit northwest'. Finding the shop was easy and her friend and I had already seen a coffee shop where we could while away our waiting time. Upon entering the salon, Lyda was greeted with grand enthusiasm and we were blatantly ignored. We didn't mind, as it was not our hair that was going to be styled anyway. So, we were off to the coffee shop in a hurry, as the owner was dismissing us with a wave of the hand.

Several cups of coffee later, and even a tour through a bookstore and gift shop, we decided she surely must be "all pretty" by this time. As we walked into the salon, I saw the red hair before I saw anything! How could anyone miss that fairly glowing color? To my shock I realized it was Lyda's hair! She shyly admitted that he had convinced her to 'go red' and if we could wait a while longer for his finishing touches? We backed out the door and scurried around the corner before we totally lost our composure. We looked at each other and said in unison, 'Do think she's going to like that bright red hair'? An hour or so later we returned; Lyda was smiling ear to ear as she finished paying and returned her credit card to her glitzy designer purse.

Checking into the Ritz was exciting for me. I had stayed at truly nice hotels in my time, but never a Ritz. I often tell people when we got to the room, we turned out the lights and Lyda's hair glowed in the dark. That's an exaggeration of course, but it did glow! The ensuing week was a total pleasure and Lyda has toned down the color since that first dye job. With the red hair, her personality changed; her blue eyes appear bluer and sparkle more than ever. She constantly receives compliments for that incredible hair.

Often men will whistle and say, "Oh I like that red hair'! Lyda comes back with a sweet smile and says, 'Thanks, it comes from a bottle'. Seeing the joy of her transformation, I have concluded that 'Bouffant Daddy' knew what was best for her all along.

Have You Ever Seen A Bee?
A poem for Chance Overbey

Have you ever seen a bee,
Cavorting with glee
Upon the flat surface
Of an open faced rose?

Moving and wriggling with complete abandon,
Could be immersing
Totally in pollen

Don't know,
Do you?
Perhaps he's just dancing the 'boogaloo'!

Have you ever passed
A glorious stand of Susan flowers,
The ones with black eyes?
And startled a flock of
Beautiful gold finch
Hiding there and blending
Within a cornucopia
Of yellow and black?

Have you ever observed
Two humming birds
Of the feminine gene
All iridescent green
Buzzing and diving
And saying dirty
Humming words
To each other?
And they're the GIRLS!
I've heard their fights
Are over territorial rights

Have you ever talked
To a praying Mantis
Those beautiful creatures
Who look like something
From lost Atlantis?
I love the way they 'pray'
And move their gentle heads
To hear just what you've said

Have you seen the little red toads
Who blend with safe abode
Right into the rocks and clay?
I'm careful when I mow
And stop when they appear
Upon my path
And let them hop away
Safe, without fear
Of my destruction

Oh the
Peace, solitude and joy
Observing them will give,
I watch them go and let them live.

The creatures abiding in our world
Are
All a portion of the grandness
Of our God

Winter and Spring of My Soul

I have fertilized the basket of African violets
They sit and bless me —strut and bloom, bask in the sunny kitchen
window on glorious days when the sun pours into the deep recesses of
a window built just for me, long ago in love.

Those violets given by Cathy friend, who tends the flowering of my
heart and often says, 'I love you, you don't judge me'. The consummate
Catholic mother, strong in her faith and loyal. She walked with me
through the winters of my soul.

Friend Ellen calls, surprised that I am driving into town on a day in
February when freezing rain came as a visitor in the night. Rising
tempts have turned it into a cold, bleak liquid. Friend Ellen who walked
with me through the winters of my soul, says 'you never poke your head
out when there is threat of ice and snow. She doesn't realize that I have
driven through more snows than she has ever seen in a lifetime. Years of
Iowa and Wisconsin winters for the love of a glorious man. I no longer
have to risk my pounding heart to danger.

Ambition will not come to me today. It matters not, for I am blessed
with warmth and comfort, planned years ago for times like these.
And just when I thought those winters of the soul would last forever,
crying out in pain and loss, along came the fair haired boy from child
hood to bring springtime to my soul. Along came new friends, old
friends, the quiet, soft spoken boy from school days, who is now a wise
'cowboy', long conversations about what we've learned and what we
continue to learn from living the winters and springs of our souls. Wine
and dinners on Wednesdays with a handsome, grand and gracious
friend who adds red, purple, blue, yellow and pink dimensions of love
and knowledge, comfort and grace to my life. The soda jerk scientist,
song writer and constant inspiring 'Memphis Man from puberty,
always there when I feel a joy or an empty space. I've learned to waltz
and tango, gracefully across a hardwood floor. The cherished boys I
so tenderly bore, have become men who protect and pamper me with

grand manly devotion. Pride in their life station brims my cup and swells this heart. This heart that has found springtime again.

I've called the company about Medicare. I do believe that's all I need to do today. The ivy is glossy on the fence and the daffodils show dark green promise. I will curl up with a good book, awaiting the call that will come from the fair-haired boy, the grand, wise man, who loves me now in a finding that amazes and delights. And so, because I can, I shall suspend myself in cozy thanksgivings.

Panorama Shores
Western Kentucky
February 5, 2004

Dragon Fly

Am truly glad
I did not know
In those tender years long ago

A fledgling child
A sensitive girl
Reveling in God's natural
World

Hours spent
Sweet content
By the pond
Where moss and algae grew

Before high heels and garter belts
Lipstick and wildly beating heart
Bringing on joy and pain of just living
Glories of nature did the giving

Oh wonder at fat tadpoles wiggling
Round the waters edge
Tiny fishes leaped in silver flashes
Winged insects skimmed
Green reflected worlds

Oh the stillness gift of sight!
Do not breathe, dragon flies alight.

A moon appears up in the sky
And mother calls
Come home
Oh I am glad I did not know
About the dragonfly – they live one day and then they die.

Hello Like Before

In describing grief and loss, I have often compared it to moving through bracken water, made muddy and unpleasant by the constant silt of time. When I had reached the plateau of those experiences and began to feel joy once more, I could hardly believe that I had survived it all. The new friends, the kind and gentle thoughtful old friends and neighbors, learning to dance, having those two sons who constantly lift up my spirit with pride and tenderness, and writing poems. At the encouragement of my daddy just before he died, I was even thinking of compiling them into a book.

There remained an insistent longing and emptiness within my heart. My youngest son explained it for me. He told me it was because his father and I had possessed such a great love. Then he said, 'Mom, stop searching, just wait upon it and it will come to you. This was the dear one who told me that every morning when I opened my eyes to say, 'I can do anything I want to do today.' I wanted another great love! Listening to a tape one day, a song I had never heard begun to play. There was Nancy Wilson singing, 'Hello Like Before'. Such a lovely musical thought to a man not seen in a long, long time. I wondered, 'where is David, how is David and oh how I'd like to sing that song to him'. I had never forgotten the stolen kiss that sent us to the principal's office all those years ago. Then I remembered that the last time I had seen him, he was living in Alabama and very much a married man. So, right out of my head went that longing thought!

My oldest had insisted I sign up for email and patiently taught me how to use the computer and begin to communicate with friends electronically. One day I received an email from the president of the class below me in school. Brian was remembering me fondly and asking if I would consider attending their reunion in June. I quickly responded back that I'd be happy to see he and all the others once again.

The evening of the reunion I drove to the meeting place and parked my car in the lot. I had just closed the door when I heard a man calling to me, 'Georgia, Sweet Georgia'. I looked across the way and there was the most handsome man! As we drew near to each other I could fairly feel the pull of desire! He took me into his arms and began talking and talking. I didn't know who he was, but I wanted to stay wrapped in that embrace forever. It felt amazingly like 'coming home again'. Then he leaned me back and looking right into my eyes with his incredible eyes, so blue/green and fairly dancing with joy. He said, 'You don't know who I am do you?' I had to admit I didn't but did not admit I didn't care so long as he just would not let me go! Then he said, 'It's David' and pulled me very close again. Then I knew why I was feeling this energy of connected 'soul, touching thrill'. It had never left us after all this passage of time. During the entire evening of renewing and hugging, it seemed as if when I turned around he was always near me. Just as we were in high school, even though we never kissed again, we formed such a special bond with each other. After that dreaded visit to the principal, who made me feel like a fallen woman with his 'fifties' morality lecture, simply because David and I had kissed in the hallway. We never kissed again. Perhaps it was because of fear and undeserved guilt. I don't think we ever knew for certain why. He even went on to fall in love with a beautiful blond, blue-eyed girl. Even so, our connection and wanting always hung between us like a beautiful gossamer ribbon.

When we said good-bye that night of the reunion, he gave me his business card and asked me to promise that we would not lose each other again. Little did he know how determined I was to keep that promise. There is a lovely blue grass song popular now called 'Be Ready To Sail. Hearing it for the first time, I concluded that it described just how I felt driving home that night. 'Be ready to sail when a good wind blows your way, cast your fate upon the water, catch a big wave by the tail, when a good wind blows your way, be ready to sail.' Intuitively, I knew David was a 'good wind blowing for me' and I eagerly 'set my sail'.

However, I was about to discover that unlike me, apparently David had doubts. We did several months of calling back and forth. Just when I would begin to think he was slipping away from me, back he'd come with a phone call or email. He had admitted that he'd spent long years in an unhappy marriage.

We seemed to magically reach a point in our time together when we both knew we had tumbled, fallen, floated deeply into love. Hours of conversation David calls 'spiritual love making', discovering that we were of like mind on everything! He often 'turned my heart over' playing his guitar, singing to me, with me, and the day he said to me, 'someone must have said a prayer for me when I found you again'. .... Oh that put me in mind of the quote from Song of Solomon; 'set me as a seal on your heart, as a seal on your arm, for as stern as death, is love.' I was his to love and cherish right then and there with no more doubts and no more questions! I felt with my whole heart as Luanne Rice says in her book Sandcastles, "I am standing on the threshold of another trembling world". There and now I knew I had crossed that beautiful 'bridge' from loss to gain. And even now, and always, as Sheri Reynolds character says in the book, The Rapture of Canaan, 'his hands felt like a remedy to all the badness I ever knew.'

Our lives are blended together but I don't want to leave the idea that everything is perfection. Occasionally there comes seemingly out of nowhere, a 'fly' to light in our 'ointment'. It is always someone or something else that provides the pebble in our road of love. Together we circumvent it. When he holds my hands in his and prays. When he asks God to bless our relationship, my heart and soul feel the wisdom and the comfort of this man.

It took a lot of effort to find, for my garden, a statue of King David. Here in the Bible belt they frown upon such things. A friend found it in a garden center in Northern Illinois and delivered it to me with a coat covering the entire five feet of the concrete structure. And I say to everyone, I had a dear sweet Prince for a special time in my life. Now, I have a dear sweet King.

And truly I am silly in love. Antoine de Saint-Exupery said, 'Love is not just looking at each other, but looking in the same direction'. I have always steadfastly believed in faith and hope. And as Reynolds says, 'I love him like the air, always moving but constant as hope'.

The following are some of my letters to my King, my David, and my love.

Gently Flow

There's a Cardinal perched
Upon my trellis where the beautiful
And bright morning glories bloom
In late summer profusion

'Blue eyes crying in the rain'
My emotions are a mass of longing
And heart filled confusion

Clouds of butterflies alight around
The base of fallen fruit by the pear tree
The sheer beauty of it
Astounds me

He is dead
You are not him and must not feel the need
To fill his empty shoes
They are not here, he took them with him
And I...have let go
You, are so much more
In many ways...that please and fill me
She is dead...to you
And even if I wished to try,
My eyes
Will never be blue
Elvis is dead
With God's blessings, our love has become a human
Amazing grace
Please tell me that you love
These hazel eyes that fill with light
At the thought of you

I am responsible for you in love,
You are responsible for me in love,
And this love we share is

A grand thing
Therefore, we forgive at first blush of recognition
When we stumble and move on to love and respect
This life is often full of heartache
But also more times full with blessing
Our finding is a grand blessing
Perhaps in heaven we will have
All that we wished in this life
Or perhaps we will accept and understand
Why it was not meant to be
Here
'We go by the light we have at the time.'
And so
I tell you in song and in rhyme
Let this love we have found
Ebb and flow
Gently between us

A Letter from Alaska

My Darling,

Oh so good to hear your voice today, to hear your thoughts and sweetness coming through each word to me!

Being here in the middle of this winter country has brought back many, many memories of all those years in Iowa and Wisconsin.

The crunch of ice and snow beneath my feet, the necessity of constantly reminding one's self to walk carefully in boot-shod feet and wool socks, for weeks and weeks. Driving on icy, snow laden roads for months. The howl of the wind and the color of long winters, brown, black and white and white on white with only evergreen to punctuate the bleakness of cold skies. The glorious welcome of sunshine, hold the preciousness of its gift shining into the window of cold. Layer upon layer of clothing and heavy coats for weeks on end. A houseplant, a blooming flower blesses the soul's spirit and lifts the tediousness of long nights and short days. For years, thirteen of them in northeast Iowa, where the names of good people were so foreign to me. Homesickness hitting like a highflying boulder out of nowhere. Only the great love of husband and children and an unmoving faith kept me sane and sound.

This is why I love my south now, my western Kentucky surroundings where I know, God willing, I will be picking and smelling daffodils in

March. A place where greening never really hides in winter. Ivy on the fence, sage in the garden. An incredible fair-haired boy of the past often comes to visit the vestigages of my mind, smiling, flirting with me. And on the phone, I close my eyes, and let the sweet sugar sounds of his Alabama accent fill my heard and fill my heart. And oh, the comfort of knowing again, my lips will feel the soft, yearning pressure of his and I can drown in the tenderness of his blue eyes, his thoughtful conversation and be moved to the edge of an emotional cliff by our give and take of feelings and ideas. Listening to music that we love and hearing his voice in song. So many blessings draw me there and hold me dearly within a tender, thankful embrace. Nikiski, Alaska January 3, 2004.

Sharing Sweetness

My darling, my love…stopped for only a moment to eat, to rest and to watch the grandness of the green out of doors. Then, remembering oh remembering the sweetness we shared just days ago. My writer mind will not let me go on with this day until these words that rest upon my heart, wing their way to you. Wishing I had remembered to tell you things I forgot when we spoke over lines of love that cannot be seen by the human eye. Have just taken in the vivid blue of the Blue Bird at the cat food again. But then, a redheaded woodpecker flew down to see what so intrigued the Blue Bird. Oh the beauty of his color! Cardinal and Wrens alike are feasting upon my unsightly compost pile. Their flights to and from make up for it's more than messy appearance to my orderly desires.

Yes, the tulips are indeed leaning toward where you sat, but I won't tell, maybe. A moment ago, was just thinking of how you react when you catch me staring at you, when our eyes meet and you say to me, 'what?' Then you know that it is only my lust for living and for enjoying and memorizing the look of you. Oh the feeling when our eyes lock in embrace while in a crowded room. Folding your undershirts from the dryer and lovingly placing them where you will find them when you are here again. Remembering how you take my hand and squeeze it in a moment of love so strong my heart can hardly take it in, but oh I do. My darling, my Babe…. you are involved with a lady so taken with life, so amazed at the wonder of it, of love, that sometimes I feel as if I cannot bear the joy and cry while locked so closely against your back, but quietly so you won't know. I long to weep openly while in your arms, but you say you don't like crying. Well darlin, my crying is different. I'm done with the sorrowful stuff and pray that it will not touch me again too soon. But if it does I'll deal with it and survive if meant to be.

Oh but I do love laughing with you! And laughing and loving is what we should strive to do most of all!

Day of Hearts

Upon this day of hearts
Set aside for love

My wish for you
Oh lovely one
A song that lingers on and on....

The beauty of dawn
The coo of a dove....

A noonday delight
A promise of springtime
And
Joyous warmth of the sun
A time for us of mirth and fun

Oh hold my hand,
In tenderness and care
I wish for you
A sunset at ending
To fill your soul
And bless your heart
And kiss your face
In friendship
And
In grace

Valentines Day 2004

Devine

I am wondering why this passionate thing that I experience
Should be

Within this God given, glorious world
Each season when the sun kisses the earth
And grasses and flowers unfurl
Each new miracle moves and amazes
But, of all these given things,
The morning glory
Ah the morning glory!
Devine
Especially the Heavenly Blue

These glories bloom late
In comparison to other beauties
And oh they are so fragile!
Each incredible blossom
Blooms for just one day
One precious morning

They cannot be plucked
And put into a crystal vase
They must be treasured
On the vine

In my poet's mind
I can compare
My love for you
Devine

Oh my handsome lover
A thought of you
A touch, a look, a kiss
Floats me to passion

Cedar Fence Rows

I find myself saving
A fragrant candle
To burn when I am with you
The all too small and precious hours
We spend together
Desiring to protect you from the world
From hurt and harm

Musing about what sumptuous
Thing I can cook that will send
Your adorable mouth to ecstasy
Pour your coffee into a thin china cup

How you plumb the depths of my soul
With your eyes
And when you pray

Oh new into our togetherness you said, 'someone said a prayer for me
when you came along.'
The very essence of you is burned within my mind like a song
And all the world's poets, including me, cannot accurately define

Conversations about the philosophical
Conversations about the trivial
Sugar drips from your southern voice
Saying ' goodnight baby'
'Hello sweetheart'
And...... 'I love you.'
Oh there are others
And they are beautiful
But they are not you
And like the morning glory,
The crystal vase,
The linen cloth,
The aged lace
You are fragile
My love

When our souls touch and blend...
You move me
To a never felt love
Not like anything before,
To unbridled
Passion
Devine

June 17, 2006

Comforting Peace

The glory and peace of this day, this morning I have spent. The only addition to make it more peaceful would be the presence of you, my love. I went to the turnip green patch and picked a huge bag of greens to freeze just in case they aren't here when you come. Hopefully they will survive a few cold snaps before giving their all to be frozen where they stand. Then picked persimmons as they plopped from the tree. Ground the pulp through the food mill. Quite a messy process but has become almost an autumn ceremony for me ---'picking persimmons when the time is right'---from 'Old Fashioned Woman'. Cooked the greens and stopped often to just take in all the beauty around me. Finally got two glorious blooms from the Heavenly Blue morning glory vine. My favorite and difficult to grow. Also saucer size white blooms from the moonflower vine. I take in each one of them as they are so beautiful…the small deep purple ones, the pale pink and almost mauve ones…for I know they will be gone with the first freeze.

Baked a dark cherry cobbler to take tonight. Of course there will be so much food.

Must clean the errant vines out of my big rose bush Ginny gave me years ago as I plan to pick up a tall metal trellis from my friend who made the gates to the courtyard for me.

Here I am in my little world with thoughts of you, surrounded by beauty and kept in comforting peace.

Georgia Carole Douglas

Anthem to the Morning -- Sunday

My Darling David,

Morning sun gently touching the deep brown water of the lake
Remembering the taste of morning coffee and your kisses

Bright, white, softly feathered gulls dip and glide across the expanse
Longing for the look of you sleeping peacefully in my bed
Longing for the touch of you warm from the recesses of night solace

Thankful for the rest and peace of home
Thankful for the knowledge that you will think of me today and
smile in love and memory

Time and circumstance seem to give and take in painful beauty
Oh how I long to rest my head upon your chest and hear that grand
heart beat

I want the physical but rest upon the spiritual
What great someone or something brought us together again?
I like to think that God in His infinite mercy smiled down and
realized the gift of our finding again and blessed us with His grace

I pray that just at this moment while I am musing in wonder
That you too, are thinking of this love, this marvelous friendship,
this joining

I love you with my whole heart, yesterday, today and tomorrow and
all the tomorrows that will come to us

Saturday Morning
March 20, 2004
First Day of spring
A Love Letter

Darling Handsome,

How I wish you were here. I'm cooking saffron rice with chopped yellow and green peppers, onion, celery and fresh parsley. Simmering in chicken broth base. A Great Blue Heron just flew over the house and I have been outside since seven this morning, cleaning my little outside 'entrance room' and playing like a little girl. The purple grape hyacinths, so tiny and beautiful, are blooming. Blossoms like twenty or more little bells hanging on a slender stem. The tiny daffodil that I gave you last year is in bloom again. On one stem two blossoms, one on top of the other, for you and I?

The anemone I wrote about in Moon Stages has pushed their way out of the ground and leaning their green faces to the sunlight. The berm to the front by the porch is buttery yellow with daffodils, their cups tossed by the wind. Those are the 'puddles of gold' I refer to in the poem 'Substance's Son'. Rod planted them for me years ago. Oh how they continue to bless my heart each springtime.

I wish you were here. I need to feel your touch on my skin, your kiss on my lips and to be held ever so dearly like you do when I tell you these things.

I love you and miss you my sweet.

'Look for me by moonlight;
Watch for me by moonlight;
I'll come to thee by moonlight,
Though hell should bar the way!'   *Alfred Noyes*

'How sweet the moonlight sleeps upon this bank!

Georgia Carole Douglas

Here we will sit and let the sounds of music
Creep in our ears; soft stillness and the night
Become the touches of sweet harmony.' William Shakespeare -- The
Merchant of Venice

'Unbridled Song'

Quiet by chance I heard a phrase voiced by
An old acquaintance of long ago days
He eloquently described a horse
In his manner, great detail
Of course

And often as I do
Listened with patience, for he has a need to 'tell'
Friends frequently say that my attributes are 'true'

When he mentioned the name
A revealing came
For
I have searched and searched ways to express
Emotions you stir
Emotions you tumble
Within my heart

'Unbridled' was the name he said
And oh the feelings that came to me!
Though many a song and many a poem
Mention this very thing about love

When I am with you and you hold my hand
As you always do
Sweetly wanting me to tag along
With you
I simply feel akin
To an unbridled song

Saturday, January 18, 2003

Sweetheart,

We have about 31/2" of snow on the ground from Thursday. I awoke to sunshine but now clouds and it's snowing again. My heart wishes for you...here in the peace so beautiful my soul sings from it!

About The Author

Georgia Carole Douglas is a native of the lake lands area of Western Kentucky. She lives in the little house her late husband gave to her years ago. The home and surrounding beauty provide a tranquil place for writing.

A sign on the back door reads, 'Poet's House' and writing poetry began for her long ago in fifth grade.

Her passions include reaching out to others in an attitude of love, writing, gardening, music, reading and ballroom dancing. She often performs readings from her two previously published books, 'Emotions of A Woman – Reflection' and 'Moon Stages'. She also does preview readings from the short story collection that culminated into this book. She truly enjoys the time spent entertaining at retirement homes, rest homes and civic clubs.

She currently serves on a legacy committee dedicated to the purpose of erecting a memorial site, a museum exhibit and website for the school she attended on the university campus in her hometown.

CPSIA information can be obtained
at www.ICGtesting.com
Printed in the USA
FFHW020618120619
52958131-58554FF

9 781434 367655